From Ratholes to Rainbows:
Managing Project Recovery

First edition: October 2007

Published in Canada by:

D2i Consulting
58 Aitken Circle
Markham, Ontario
L3R 7L2
Canada
Tel: (905) 475-9285

email: info@D2i.ca

website: www.D2i.ca

The authors can also be reached at: Kothari@D2i.ca

ISBN 0-9780469-1-0

This book is available at special quantity discounts for bulk purchases for corporate promotions, training or educational use. Additional materials including the AIM Methodology Handbook with the A10 Recovery Processes, customized workshops and project management templates can be ordered from the publisher.

Other books published by D2i Consulting

Rainbows & Ratholes:
Best Practices for Managing Successful Projects
Author: Dhanu M Kothari
ISBN: 0-97804-69000-1; ISBN-13: 978-1419646010

Dedicated to .....

Neela and Priya Kothari

and

Althea and Ethan Mitchell

Your enthusiastic support
and encouragement
made this book
a reality.

acknowledgements

This book was only made possible with the enthusiastic support of family, friends, clients and colleagues who shared with us a passion for Project Management. Without their constant encouragement, it would have forever remained an "unfinished project awaiting completion" or more appropriately, "a troubled project awaiting recovery".

We are deeply indebted to friends and colleagues who provided valuable insight by sharing experiences, challenging assumptions and formulating ideas for this book.

We extend a special "thank you" to industry experts, professionals and clients from government and industry organizations, and to members of the Project Management Institute (PMI) Chapters in Canada, many of whom have adopted the various models described in this book and made helpful suggestions to enhance them.

The acknowledgements would not be complete without a very special "Thank You" to our families - Neela and Priya Kothari, and Althea and Ethan Mitchell respectively - for sacrificing their leisure hours to let us work on this project.

Rajini Comfort patiently reviewed the manuscript and provided guidance during its development and editing. Thank you Rajini for your guidance and patience!

Dhanu M Kothari
Romeo Mitchell
Toronto, Canada

October 28, 2007

The journey to a

successful recovery

begins with accepting that

the project is in trouble.

From Ratholes to Rainbows:
Managing Project Recovery

Table of Contents   Page

Managing Recovery with the A^{10} Processes

00   introduction

Project Management encompasses almost everything that we do, locally and globally, whether we know it or not. In our day to day lives, projects encompass most of our endeavours such as exploring space travel, constructing nuclear power plants, building water filtration systems, conducting heart bypass surgeries, rolling out complex computer systems, managing election campaigns, completing mergers and acquisitions, and launching new products and services. Even in our personal lives, we are surrounded by examples of projects that include pursuing college education, planning an event, or renovating kitchens and basements.

Projects enable us to translate our vision into reality.

Many of these projects seldom go according to plan, but instead go "haywire". Dozens of reports published every year by industry analysts and public sector auditors around the world bear ample evidence of failing, failed or flopped projects.

These projects continue to experience the challenge of missed deadlines, budget overruns, unacceptable performance and poor customer satisfaction. They begin to impact a project team's capacity, confidence and credibility by slowly giving rise to panic and pessimism in the organization, and create a sense of failure.

Such projects are commonly referred to as "troubled" projects, and they are associated with the expression **"The project is in a rathole"**. They are waiting to be recovered, rescued and salvaged or, when everything else fails, terminated. The group of professionals who specialize in turning around a troubled project and bringing it under control are known as Project Recovery Managers. Hence, the title of the book "From Ratholes to Rainbows: Managing Project Recovery".

Turning a troubled project around is a much more difficult task than running a routine project. There are the challenges of wrestling with an overwhelming sense of pessimism and low morale among project team members. Time is of the essence in demonstrating recovery, and there is a sense of urgency combined with a high expectation of results to demonstrate that the project is back to normal and under control.

A successful recovery can only be achieved by a Project Manager who has the right approach, skills and competencies supported by extensive experience, knowledge, tools and techniques for Project Recovery Management.

This book is a result of an inquiry into the methods and mindset of the successful Project Recovery Manager. How is Project Recovery Management different from conventional Project Management practices? What makes one an effective Recovery Manager? What are the principles and practices that are commonly adopted by the successful Recovery Manager? The inquiry and associated research culminated into the development of a simple model, presented in this book as the "A^{10} Model" for project recovery.

This book is organized into 6 chapters. Chapter 1 presents a view of the world of recovery management, while Chapter 2 describes the various options and alternatives for decision making with respect to recovery. Chapter 3 deals with the skills and competencies of a Recovery Manager. Chapter 4 describes the Audit - Implement - Manage (AIM) methodology for recovery and introduces the A^{10} model for recovery.

Chapters 5 to 14 provide a detailed description of each of the ten processes and related methods and tools. They also serve as the foundation for a more detailed recovery methodology published by the authors. Chapter 15 summarizes the best practices for managing a recovery and Chapter 16 presents a realistic case study involving a large multi-national organization where the concepts outlined in this book were successfully applied. A set of templates based on best practices for managing project recovery and projects in general, is provided in the Appendix.

It is our sincere hope that professionals at all levels and in various functions of management including executives, engineers, project managers, systems analysts, client representatives, team members and students of Project Management will find this book useful towards managing difficult project situations and avoiding them, if at all possible.

For those who are relatively new to Project Management, we recommend that they refer to the following book to get familiar with basic principles and terminology: "Rainbows & Ratholes: Best Practices for Managing Successful Projects" by Dhanu Kothari.

Successful project recovery is achieved through dedicated customer focus, committed sponsorship, trusting relationships, outstanding teamwork and continuous improvement.

A failed recovery, on the other hand, points to one or more of the following ten failures in the organization:

Failure to Accept the fact, **Failure to Assess** the project, **Failure to Adapt** project objectives to business needs, **Failure to Assign** responsibilities and delegate, **Failure to Achieve** goals by setting targets, **Failure to Act** consistently and decisively, **Failure to Advance** the project through communications, **Failure to Accomplish** stability for turnover, **Failure to Alter** project direction through effective transition, and **Failure to Align** for on-going project execution.

Any of these failures will drive a project back into a rathole. You can get your project out of the rathole, or better still, avoid it completely, and catch the pot of gold at the end of the rainbow with the ideas described in this book.

Here's to managing a successful project recovery!

Dhanu Kothari
Romeo Mitchell

October 28, 2007

01

the world of
troubled projects

The history of Project Management is replete with examples of troubled and failed projects. There is ample evidence of troubled projects leading to monumental failures in all aspects of industry and government, ranging from abandoned IT projects, failed company mergers and inadequate responses to natural disasters, to space missions that ended in tragedies.

In each of these cases, the need for project recovery was not recognized. Failing to recognize the need for project recovery ultimately guarantees the failure of a project. Failure begins with a lack or denial of recognizing and accepting a "troubled" state in a project. It is seldom caused by unknown or mysterious factors surrounding a project. It is predictable, based on symptoms and warning signs in a project. And it can be prevented, by following a disciplined approach to recover the project.

A project that shows the symptoms of being in trouble is labeled as "A project headed for a rathole". In its troubled state, it oscillates like a pendulum between two danger zones - it's either Fouled Up Beyond Belief (FUBB) or Fouled Up Beyond Repair (FUBR)! Either one of those situations will result in low morale, burn out, distrust, damaging stress and destructive conflicts, leading to project failure.

The purpose of Project Recovery is to prevent project failure, and the professionals who manage recovery are known as Project Recovery Managers (PRM). It is their job to manoeuvre the project and steer it skillfully to bring it within control, and achieve the intended project outcome. This can only be accomplished by having a consistent and proven process for managing project recovery.

What is a Troubled Project?

The journey to recovery begins with the acceptance that a project is in trouble. There are many definitions and perspectives of a troubled project depending upon the various stakeholders and their attitudes, interests, influences and vulnerability regarding the project. As an example, a client might be utterly dissatisfied and frustrated with the pace of progress or quality of deliverables, while the Project Manager honestly believes that everything is on schedule, especially from a technical perspective, and anything else that affects the project is simply the client's fault. The impact of such issues, if they are allowed to simmer with no attempt at resolution, can be devastating.

A simple way of looking at a troubled project is from the client's or customer's perspective. A project is in trouble when there is a continued and sustained pattern of failure with respect to meeting the client's expectations as illustrated in the Project Recovery Zone (Figure 1). These failures usually manifest themselves as schedule slippages, budget overruns, missed deliverables, unacceptable quality or performance issues, a sense of general malaise among team members and overall client disillusionment with the project.

There is a need, however, to differentiate between a truly troubled state of a project and the day to day, routine variances that usually occur on any project. Sometimes the routine variances may appear to be quite complex and challenging because of constraints and dynamics associated with the project. A project under these circumstances could be considered as being difficult, but not necessarily a "troubled" one.

Failure to meet business objectives is a key characteristic of a troubled project. Quite often, the business objectives themselves are not understood due to lack of a business case, a project charter and a project plan.

Criteria for Troubled Projects

There are two sets of criteria for troubled projects: Objective Criteria and Subjective Criteria. Objective criteria serve as hard measures relative to project performance, and they are usually defined in the context of industry, organization and type of project. Subjective criteria are a function of variable and human factors with respect to a specific project. The following examples illustrate the difference between the two criteria.

Figure 1

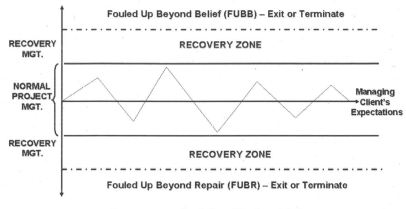

Project Recovery Zone

Is your project "just in trouble" or
Is it really a "troubled" project?

© Dhanu Kothari & Romeo Mitchell 2007

Objective Criteria

The objective criteria for troubled projects are defined by the triple constraints of Cost, Time and Performance. Here are some guidelines to serve as warning signals if your project is showing a trend towards:

- 30% or more over estimated budget (Cost)
- 30% or more over estimated target date (Time)
- 30% or more over estimated resources (Performance)
- Repeated failure to complete deliverables (Performance)
- Repeated failure to meet the client's quality standards (Performance)

The suggested guidelines will need to be adapted to different circumstances depending upon the type of industry, nature of project and acceptable variations. In the absence of an understanding and timely assessment of these trends, it is highly likely that a successful project recovery will not happen.

Subjective Criteria

The subjective criteria for troubled projects consist of Variable factors and Human factors. The variable factors are indicated by the presence of the following:

1. The integrity and value of deliverables, as perceived by the client, are questionable. The client fails to see the benefits or value of the deliverables.

2. There is a lack of acknowledgement of risks associated with the project, and there are no plans for managing project risks. The project is driven by a deadline; therefore, there is no room for risks.

3. There is an inherent mismatch in terms of goals, constraints and promises associated with the project. The project objectives are neither realistic nor achievable.

4. There is a lack of alignment and consistency in procurement strategy in relation to the overall project constraints. The project is defined as "fixed price" while critical suppliers are working on a "time and materials" or "pay as you go" basis.

Human factors for troubled projects include fragile stakeholder and team relationships, dissatisfied clients, dysfunctional communication, lack of purpose, non-existent or poor documentation, language of despair, and talk of legal action among involved parties. These are often evident as symptoms that serve as early warning signs for troubled projects. Figure 1 illustrates the difference between a project that is operating under normal, steady conditions and a project trend towards failure.

The Slippery Slope to Troubled Projects

There are many factors that could lead a project into a troubled state. Here's the "dirty dozen" list that is primarily associated with troubled projects. Note that none of the following present themselves as a one-time or unexpected events - rather, they tend to accumulate over time and push the project to operate in a troubled mode. They are also associated mostly with people and communication issues rather than product, process and technology considerations.

1. Failure to recognize the symptoms of trouble
2. No sponsorship & management commitment
3. Project "hijacked" by promise of technology and technologists
4. Lack of focus on business process and strategy
5. Force-fitting a technical solution for every business problem
6. Lack of rationale and acceptance criteria for requirements
7. Project objectives lost in change control & issue management
8. Wishful thinking; Hiding of problems; Culture of fear; Outright lies
9. Lack of Business Case, Project Charter and Project Plan
10. Lack of awareness, assessment and planning for project risks
11. Poor communication both within and outside the team
12. Poor Management of Change and Cultural Integration

Recovering from a Troubled Project

An understanding of issues surrounding project failures provides an insight into what needs to be done to achieve a successful recovery. The major issues, as summarized below, relate to project alignment, interfaces, objectives, organization and the management of change.

1. Project objectives are not aligned with business goals and strategies. There is the need to evaluate and realign objectives which will form the basis for the initial recovery strategy.

2. There are many interfaces and points of failure that derail the project due to interpretation and complexity of communication. The seeds of failure can germinate anywhere throughout the project cycle starting with Business Needs and progressing through Requirements, Specifications, Design, Development, Test and the Final Outcome. Developing an understanding of the interfaces and communication needs is essential for the recovery process.

3. Project objectives have not kept pace with business needs that often change since the project started. Projects are often associated with intangible benefits and varying cross-functional roles and expectations, thereby leading to the perception of failure. Staying focused on the changing business needs and integrating them into the project through a formal change control process is critical to recovery.

4. Projects encompass more than just the delivery organization. The dynamics and politics among various stakeholders and parts of the organization can result in weakening the project, if left unchecked. Understanding the involvement of stakeholders should include the interests of individuals as well as business groups and organizations that could have an impact on the project.

5. "Management of Change" is the single most important factor that is often overlooked during planning. It has to do with getting people ready and trained so that they are willing to embrace people and process-related changes resulting from

the project. Change implications of projects are generally underestimated or not considered at all from a "management of change" perspective.

Project failures can be prevented by taking timely steps for project recovery. Such recovery is essentially an intervention by the Project Recovery Manager to help the team to bring it under control and stabilize it for further progress. The Recovery Manager has several options including redefining the project, resetting expectations, reorganizing the team and reforming project management practices – that ultimately lead to project success.

Key Concepts and Terminology

☐ *Assessment*

The structured review of the project and project plans. It is similar to what the Project Management Institute (PMI) calls an audit. An assessment results in a review of possible options and recommendations for a "Go Forward" plan.

☐ *Business Value*

Business Value is measured by the extent to which a project's outcomes can be directly linked with its contribution to an organization's strategies and business goals related to improved customer satisfaction, increased revenues, improved profits and reduced costs.

☐ *Completion Criteria*

It specifies the conditions and processes for acceptance of all of the project deliverables, and transfer of responsibility from the Project Manager to another function for ongoing operation of the project.

☐ *Exit Strategy*

Describes the conditions and criteria that would be considered, to decide if a project will be abandoned or terminated, and an orderly process for termination. As part of the strategy, the decision to terminate is followed by a communication plan to facilitate orderly termination.

☐ *Re-architect*

Re-architecture is required when business or technology conditions have changed so much that they render the current solution obsolete. Usually it is initiated as a brand new project leading to a total recovery of the project.

☐ *Recovery*

The process of bringing a troubled project under control with the objective of delivering the original or modified project outcomes that will meet the client's business needs. This is also referred to as Project Rescue or Salvage depending upon the scope and magnitude of recovery.

☐ *Termination*

Decision to stop further work and withdraw further investment into the project. This is usually a "business" decision as opposed to a "project" decision, and it is taken as a result of assessment. It may be the right thing to do if the project circumstances have changed drastically, and the business value of the project is questionable.

☐ *Troubled project*

A project that exhibits a continued and sustained pattern of failure to meet the expectations of its clients and stakeholders, and is trending towards unacceptable levels of tolerances with respect to established criteria for the triple constraints of scope, cost and time.

☐ *Turnaround (Rapid)*

Rapid turnaround is associated with projects of relatively high risks and extremely short durations. The success of these projects depends on meticulous planning using CPM tools. Because of the critical nature and short durations, project recovery is accomplished quickly through contingency planning.

☐ *Turnaround (Company)*

An organization-wide initiative that deals with changing the financial performance of a company, implementing a new business strategy, restructuring of operations, and driving cultural changes across the organization. It consists of several inter-related projects and the timeframe for such projects is usually 9-12 months.

02

dealing with troubled projects

The Project Recovery Spectrum

Ignoring a troubled project is not an option. Issues must be dealt with, lest they turn into failed projects. There are several options and strategies for dealing with troubled projects, and they are influenced by the scope and type of recovery, strategic importance and organization impact with respect to business value of the project, complexity of the solution and, finally, costs associated with the recovery.

The Project Recovery Spectrum illustrated in Figure 2-A shows four categories of recovery along with associated scope and approximate timeframes. They are: Short Term Turnaround & Recovery, Partial Project Recovery, Total Project Recovery and Program Recovery.

Options for Recovery

Short Term Turnaround

Short term turnaround projects are characterized by short durations ranging from days to weeks, quick execution, detailed planning, high risk and high impact of failure. Typical examples of these projects include moving or relocating entire company staff, conducting plant or equipment maintenance, performing network upgrades and migrating systems and applications. The objective is to have everything operationally ready and running smoothly immediately after the turnaround. Recovery in these projects is built into project plans as part of risk assessment and contingencies, and it happens during the turnaround as required.

Partial Project Recovery

The purpose of partial recovery is to rescue a troubled project with the objective of stabilizing it for further operation while salvaging as much as possible. A partial recovery can happen only if there are demonstrable business benefits, trusting relationships among all the players and willingness to achieve recovery.

In these situations, the Recovery Manager works with the project team towards establishing confidence and credibility with stakeholders, introduces appropriate practices and procedures to bring stability to the project, and coaches the entire team to regain control of the project.

Recovery is considered to be complete, when responsibility for the project is transferred back to the original Project Manager. Typical duration of recovery process lasts from 2-4 months.

Figure 2-A

The Recovery Spectrum

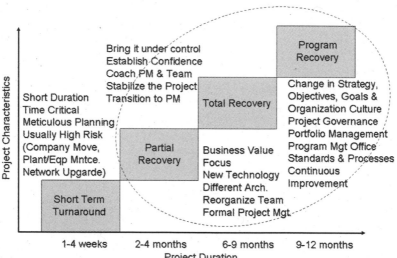

© Dhanu Kothari & Romeo Mitchell 2007

16

Total Project Recovery

Total Recovery is called for whenever there is a serious mismatch of project objectives and organizational goals. This can happen due to many reasons: lack of alignment of project objectives, changes in underlying technologies selected for the project, new business focus and a different expectation of business value.

In such cases, the options for recovery include redefining the project with a total redesign and re-architecture of the solution, and reorganizing the team. Total Recovery projects span over 4-6 months or more, and they should be treated as brand new projects along with the formal assignment of a Project Manager. The Recovery Manager's role in these projects is generally to act as a sounding board and provide coaching and mentoring to the Project Manager.

Program Recovery

Program Recovery refers to establishing Program Governance linking to Project Portfolio Management (PPM), Project Management Office (PMO), standardized methodologies and tools, and a foundation for achieving continuous improvement. The objective of program recovery is to establish policies and practices that will eliminate, or at least minimize, the recurrence of troubled projects.

Program Recovery addresses all parts of the organization as a whole, and its scope is comparable to a corporate turnaround that involves a change of business strategy, direction, culture, or organizational structure.

Recovery Strategies

There are many strategies for recovering a project. One can bleed it, kill it, mothball it, rescue it or salvage it - depending on many considerations. A recovery may, sometimes, consist of planning a graceful retreat which can be perceived as a "successful failure", or it might result in a limited or partial recovery and be perceived as a "failed success".

The decision criteria for recovery strategies is based on two considerations: (1) Business Value & Strategic Relevance of the project and (2) Cost and Complexity of Recovery

Business Value and Strategic Relevance

The first consideration in deciding about alternative approaches to recovery is the project's business value and strategic relevance to the organization. The concept of business value helps us to ask key questions surrounding the rationale and justification for doing the project in the first place.

It focuses on the project's outcome and its contribution to basic business measures such as increase in customer satisfaction, market share, profit, productivity and revenue, or decrease in costs related to distribution, inventory, marketing and manufacturing etc.

The extent to which a project's outcome can be directly linked with its contribution to an organization's business goals is a measure of its business value. The measures may vary depending upon the type of an organization, but the concept still applies whether it's a commercial enterprise, a defense organization, a government or public sector entity, a non-profit group or a volunteer organization.

Business value validates the reason for doing the project, and it provides an objective basis for assigning priorities among competing projects. It is also an effective way to get the enthusiastic support of the project sponsor and stakeholders.

Cost Considerations

The second consideration in deciding a recovery strategy is the cost and complexity of doing the recovery. Some of the questions that need to be answered are:

☐ How much will the recovery cost in terms of additional resources, both human and non-human?

☐ How long will it take to achieve the recovery and will the time-frame be acceptable to the business or the client?

☐ What's the level of complexity in terms of integration, interfaces and technologies?

☐ What are the risks associated with the recovery and can they be reasonably managed?

☐ Are the goals of recovery achievable and realistic? And finally, how desperately is the recovery needed?

A Recovery Decision Matrix is an excellent tool that provides a combined perspective of a project's business value and costs associated with recovery.

Figure 2-B

Dealing with Troubled Projects
Recovery Decision Matrix

Recovery Decision Matrix

The Recovery Decision Matrix shown in Figure 2-B illustrates the various options for recovery based on business value, strategic relevance, cost and complexity factors.

There are four options that serve as guidelines for recovery, and they are: (1) Exit (2) Reprioritize (3) Salvage and (4) Transform. Listed below are the key considerations associated with each option.

Exit or Terminate

Exiting or Termination is the best option when rescuing a project is neither desirable nor possible due to one or more of the following factors:

- The business benefits associated with the project cannot be achieved.

- Key stakeholders and the client organization are no longer supportive of the project.
- The sponsor has lost interest in the project and is no longer prepared to support it.

- The market conditions have changed and the business needs that the project is trying to satisfy are no longer valid.

- The proposed deliverables have become obsolete due to major technological changes.

- Litigation cannot be avoided or is in process.

Experienced Project Recovery Managers aim for a graceful exit with a proper plan and exit strategy.

Reprioritize

The second option is to reprioritize the project and redefine it, if necessary. The following factors influence the choice of this strategy:

- There is no compelling case for doing the project.

- The business value and strategic importance of the project is low in relation to other projects.

- The stakeholders' assessment of priority and interest has significantly diminished since the project started.

- No one is willing to act as sponsor for the project while everyone believes that it would be nice to get it done.

- The project could be undertaken as part of a larger project at a later stage.

Salvage

The third option is to salvage the project through partial recovery or rescue. Major considerations for this option are:

- The project continues to be strategically important to the organization.

- The project is expected to deliver business value following recovery.

- The project's overall approach to the solution and design architecture is still valid.

- Most of the project investment can be saved and most of the deliverables and results can be adapted for recovery.

- Management and the project team are genuinely interested in project recovery.

- An experienced Project Recovery Manager with the required skills and competencies is available for managing recovery.

The remaining chapters deal in great depth with the "Salvage" option since Recovery and Salvaging is the focus of this book.

Transform

The final option is to completely transform the project into a new one through re-definition, re-scoping, redesign and re-architecture. This option is influenced by the following factors:

- Current solution does not meet business needs.

- There are major changes in business strategy and market conditions that have resulted in new or different business needs.

- The underlying technology, components and approach to solution design are no longer valid or realistic due to changes, obsolescence or new alternatives.

- The project assumptions are no longer valid, verifiable or viable.

- Simply Exiting, Reprioritizing or Salvaging the project is NOT an option.

In this case, the newly defined project is no longer considered to be a recovery project. It is managed as a regular project in accordance with the company's standard Project Management methodology and processes.

03   the project recovery manager

The Challenge of Recovery

Recovery of a "troubled" project involves managing the project and its problems to bring it back to a stable state. The process is time consuming and requires a special set of skills. The problems of the project are often compounded by the project's sponsors from both the delivery and client organizations.

They give rise to tension between project sponsors, clients, project teams and sub-contractors resulting in the ritual of "Blame Game" and destructive politics. The project is in trouble because "it's someone else's fault", "the technology is no good", "the client doesn't know what he needs" or "we don't have enough resources" ... so goes the argument.

There is often significant resistance to accepting the need for a recovery role as it is perceived as something being thrust upon the team. The Recovery Project Manager has to deal with many perceptions, misconceptions and myths associated with the role. This is where the Recovery Manager's experience and expertise become critical to the process.

As a general practice, Recovery Managers are often brought in as interim project managers with the objective of helping the existing project manager. They assess the situation, identify corrective measures, institute formal processes, reestablish confidence, coach the Project Manager and steer the troubled project to safety. They act as catalysts to change to accomplish the recovery.

How the Recovery Manager Operates

The recovery specialist brings a fresh and independent perspective towards the understanding of troubled situations, and provides an objective assessment and evaluation of the project circumstances. The Recovery Manager's first task is to establish a sense of confidence and credibility with all stakeholders. Typical issues that the Recovery Manager needs to address right away are listed below:

- Is the management willing, ready and interested in recovering the project?

- Are the project sponsors committed to participate in the recovery?

- Will they support the Recovery Manager as being the catalyst to the recovery?

- Are there any pre-conceived ideas or expectations from the recovery?

- Can a satisfactory recovery be realistically achieved?

- Is the timeframe for partial/total reovery acceptable to sponsors & management?

- What can be reasonably and realistically expected from the recovery specialist?

- Have project issues been isolated from personal issues of the sponsors?

- Is management open to ideas/suggestions to accomplish the recovery?

- Is it acknowledged that the recovery specialist is assigned on an interim basis?

Many troubled projects can be traced to systemic problems or severe root causes in the organization. However, the Recovery Manager's primary goal is to fix the project first and get a handle on it, rather than trying to solve the organization's problems. Included in the responsibility is the aspect of financial management of the project along with the development of a realistic financial plan.

Roles & Responsibilities

A Recovery Manager must be fully knowledgeable about the conventional functions, roles and responsibilities of Project Management, and experienced in applying all of the associated processes for managing the scope, time, cost, human resources, risk, communication, procurement, quality and integration activities. However, a recovery effort is quite different from day to day conventional Project Management, and it is associated with additional responsibilities that are over and above those of the Project Manager, and are explicitly required for the recovery role. They are:

- Gain acceptance that the project is in trouble
- Identify the indicators of project health
- Understand early signs of project problems
- Assess project problems
- Identify the root cause of problems
- Develop a realistic recovery plan
- Sell the project recovery plan
- Institute formal PM discipline & processes
- Gain control over scope-creep
- Improve product quality
- Meet commitments or renegotiate them
- Actively mitigate project risks
- Make value of deliverables visible to stakeholders
- Manage and lead the project recovery
- Make the project environment stable
- Create confidence and keep the momentum going
- Communicate problems and recovery status

Skills & Competencies

Recovery Managers also have a unique set of skills and competencies that set them apart from the conventional Project Manager. They are expected to be objective in their recommendations and they have explicit authority to speak up. Some of the basic Project Management skills are more intensified and refined, while there are several others that are distinct and specific to the role of recovery. They are:

- Ability to drive down into details - but still able to see the big picture
- Flexibility and open-mindedness
- Ability to listen to different stories and viewpoints
- Ability to analyze, synthesize & draw conclusions
- Well versed in using different analytical tools
- Bias towards action
- Speak frankly while respecting confidentiality
- Willing to take career risks and lead a voyage of discovery
- Knowledge of best practices and methodologies, Project Management experience
- Significantly high capacity to absorb a lot of information
- Capable of focusing on business needs and objectives
- Differentiate between task mgt. and expectation mgt.
- Capable of adopting new Project Management techniques
- Capable of being decisive
- Focus on strategic needs, expectation setting and outcomes-based management
- Capable of handling significant stress; must be patient and a keen listener
- Must enjoy what they are doing

Behavioural Characteristics

A Recovery Manager must also exhibit the behaviour that is consistent with the roles and responsibilities, and skills and competencies that define the job. His actions are characterized by the following:

1. Bringing out hidden problems to the surface and discussing them openly.
2. Challenging arbitrary deadlines & inadequate resources.
3. Coaching the Project Manager and team members.
4. Confronting unacceptable priorities, problems and situations.
5. Exercising their explicit authority to speak up without reservations.
6. Focusing on risk management and having a risk plan.
7. Instituting an effective decision making process.
8. Practicing processes to promote good team interaction and behaviour.
9. Respecting confidentiality of clients and stakeholders.
10. Taking delight in rescuing a troubled project.

This behaviour is demonstrated by the Recovery Manager's ability to make informed decisions, gain stakeholders' acceptance, deliver quick wins, filter the noise, separate fact from fiction, generate confidence, insulate the team from internal politics, promote open communication, remove fear of failure, motivate the team and have a singular focus on the recovery.

The Outstanding Recovery Manager

The outstanding Recovery Manager must have the required skills, competencies and flexibility to quickly adapt to changing project environment as it relates to Project Management, Business Knowledge and Technology Awareness.

The Recovery role demands that the Project manager is also capable of acting confidently as a communicator, facilitator, implementer, mediator and a change agent. When it comes to Project Management competencies, the Recovery Manager is also an expert Project Manager who practices what he preaches, sets an example for others to follow and "Walks the Talk".

From a business perspective, the Recovery Manager should be able to quickly grasp the challenges, business drivers, strategies and terminology associated with the client's business, and their context and influence on the troubled project.

Without an understanding of the business basics, the Recovery Manager will barely succeed in establishing rapport with stakeholders and selling them on the objectives of recovery. When it comes to the business aspect of recovery, the Recovery Manager should "Know the Talk".

Technology awareness is the third component of competency. Managing recovery, for the most part, is concerned with people and process management. As such, the Recovery Manager needs to have a broad understanding of the technologies involved, and their capabilities and limitations relative to the project.

It is the individual project team members who have in-depth knowledge and expertise of technical aspects, and the Recovery Manager works with them to resolve technical issues. It is expected that the Recovery Manager knows how to "Talk the Talk" and understand the language of technology.

Effective communication requires using the right language and terminology that is clearly and easily understood by stakeholders and the project team. That includes the language of Project Management, the language of business or organization, and the language of the science, discipline or technology related to the project.

Figure 3 illustrates the changing and enhanced role of the Project Recovery Manager and expectations arising from the new role that encompasses Project Management, Business Awareness and Technology competencies.

Figure 3
Recovery Manager - Skills & Competencies

- Breadth and Depth of PM Experience
- Consultative and Decision Making Skills
- In-depth knowledge of Best Practices
- Outstanding Coach, Mentor and Influencer
- Bias towards Action

© Dhanu Kothari & Romeo Mitchell 2007

Recovery Outcomes

There are a number of potential outcomes that could result from trying to rescue a troubled project.

☐ Recovery is successful

New expectations are set and met through a partial or total recovery. The most important measures of a successful recovery are: stakeholder and customer satisfaction; meeting interim schedules as promised; delivering within cost and budget constraints; providing functionality as negotiated for the recovery; delivering Quality as it applies to the product and Project Management process; ensuring business value as expressed in terms of ROI or similar, and finally, establishing a sense of pride and accomplishment in the team.

☐ Recovery is ongoing and prolonged

Sometimes a slow and prolonged recovery may be the only acceptable alternative due to business and project constraints. This outcome has severe disadvantages, the primary one being that the project might suffer from the "Death by a thousand cuts" syndrome resulting in eventual termination.

Slow recovery has a negative impact on stakeholders' expectations and team morale and employee motivation. The interim Recovery Manager has a limited role in such situations, and it may consist of setting up a recovery plan to be followed by the assigned Project Manager.

☐ Recovery is a failure

In this scenario, new expectations are set and missed, thereby resulting in the failure of recovery. There are several causes that would lead to this situation. The objectives of recovery may not be achievable; the schedule may not be realistic; the costs may be unacceptable; the root causes may not be understood or resolved; or the interest in achieving recovery may have slowly diminished.

All of the classic reasons for project failure come into play in such a scenario, and ultimately they show up as Project Management issues. The failure may result in the project being cancelled or terminated

Regardless of the desired or expected outcome, it should be recognized that the work of recovery is a project by itself. It has a start and an end, milestones, deliverables, resources and risks … all the makings of a conventional project that require a consistent approach and methodology for planning, executing and implementing it. The roadmap described in the next chapter shows the way to manage a successful project recovery.

04   roadmap for recovery

The roadmap for recovery consists of two parallel paths: Project Recovery Cycle and Recovery Coaching Cycle. The first one gets the project back on track, while the second one builds the foundation for avoiding future occurrences of the need for recovery.

Just as in a relay race, the Project Recovery Manager sets the winning conditions, guides the team, leads the recovery effort and then passes on the baton to the project team who runs with it to the finish line.

The first step in setting the winning conditions is to get a high level overview of the project situation and understand the challenge and complexity of what one is faced with. This is accomplished through the Project Quick-Scan.

Project Quick-Scan

The objective of the Quick-Scan is to understand the scope and complexity of what one is dealing with and get the project profile quickly for deciding a further course of action. Prior to initiating a quick-scan it is recommended that a short questionnaire be developed with the objective of getting an understanding of major symptoms.

The Quick-Scan will demonstrate the extent to which critical information, that would influence strategy and decision making about the project, is unknown or misunderstood by key stakeholders.

This also helps the Recovery Manager to determine the information to focus on during the Quick-Scan, and begin to identify potential root cause in support of the realization of the first step in the recovery process. There are three types of quick-scans that should be conducted as a minimum prerequisite:

1. The project characteristics quick scan (PCQS) captures the key attributes about the project. It is intended for discussion with the Project Manager and the project team.

2. The Standards Compliance Quick Scan (SCQS) validates the extent to which the project is using minimum acceptable standards and formal practices for project implementation. It is used for discussions with audit and compliance functions.

3. The Business Compliance Quick-Scan (BCQS) interprets the business rationale, project strategy and other qualitative aspects related to business alignment and some of the challenges encountered by the implementation team. It is designed to facilitate discussion with senior management.

These quick scans provide multiple perspectives from different sources and give insights into why the project is in its current troubled state. Moreover, they generate credible input to accepting the fact that the project is in need of a recovery.

Typical questions for a Quick-Scan include the following:

- What is the situation?

- What are we dealing with in this project?

- What is the strategic importance and purpose of the project?

- What is the project category or type? (e.g. Routine Maintenance, Short Turnaround, Regular, Breakthrough, Research and Development etc.)
- What is the complexity of the project in terms of Size, Scale, Interfaces, Suppliers, and Geographical Spread?
- What is the technology used? Is it proven, new, tested or untested?
- How critical is the project deadline? Is it absolute - as in the case of the Olympic Games or is it relative - as in the case of a product launch?
- What are the key resources and how is the project organized?

- What is the level of readiness for risk in terms of risk awareness, risk profile and risk planning?
- What is the degree of overall confidence in terms of getting the job done? How bad is the situation?

- What are the reasons for saving the project?
- Is the project viable? Can it be saved?

The Recovery Manager discusses these questions openly with his/her client. The objective is to address them honestly, openly and quickly in order to validate that the potential for recovery exists and the management is seriously interested in achieving a successful recovery. The Quick-Scan provides crucial clues to determine if the recovery should be undertaken, and if so, it defines the broader scope of the engagement.

Planning for Recovery

The process of recovery consists of several stages: Fact-finding, Recovery Charter, Analysis, Implementation and Transition as illustrated in Figure 4-A.

1. **Fact-finding**

   A Project Recovery Manager is assigned to the project. Fact-finding is accomplished through an Initial Quick-Scan (IQS) where the objective is to learn as much as possible and as quickly as possible, to assess the present circumstances of the project. The purpose of the IQS is similar to conducting a preliminary survey to get the lay of the land. It helps the Recovery Manager to quickly look for symptoms and gauge their severity.

2. **Recovery Charter**

   The Initial Quick-Scan is followed by a Recovery Charter that outlines the business case, recommendations, and details of recovery scope, cost, resources and risks for management approval. The approved Charter validates the scope of work to be done and it authorizes the interim Project Recovery Manager to develop and implement a recovery plan.

3. **Analysis of the facts**

   This consists of conducting a series of detailed Quick Scans for project characteristics, business and standards compliance, and a formal assessment of the project using

33

various tools such as Project Health-Check, Stakeholder Analysis, Risk Profiling, Problem Solving, Root Cause Analysis and Documentation Reviews. The Health Check provides a measure of stability for the overall project and highlights the weakest elements of the project.

Figure 4-A

The Recovery Process

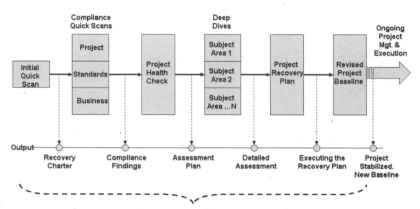

Recovery Management

© Dhanu Kothari & Romeo Mitchell 2007

4. Deep Dives

The analysis is then followed by a series of "Deep Dives" which are focused investigations into specific weak areas of the project. The results of the analysis and "deep dives" are summarized into an Assessment which includes recommendations on how to rescue the troubled project by addressing the causes of the original problem.

5. Implementation

This consists of putting the recovery plan into place, and executing the detailed steps in the recovery plan. The Recovery Manager works with the assigned Project Manager and team to implement the plan, monitor its progress and control it.

6. Stabilization and Transition

The Recovery Manager stays involved in the engagement until the project has achieved stabilization and then turns it back to the Project Manager through an orderly transition process. At this point, the project is under control, there is a new baseline for the project and the project team continues to deliver in accordance with the new baseline.

Recovery Phases and Stages

The process for recovery is divided into ten stages and grouped under three distinct phases of the recovery lifecycle. Stages 1-3 of the recovery process can be grouped and termed as *"Audit and Planning" phase (A)*, stages 4-7 as *"Implementation" phase (I)* and stages 8-10 as *"Managing the Transition" phase (M)*.

Figure 4-B

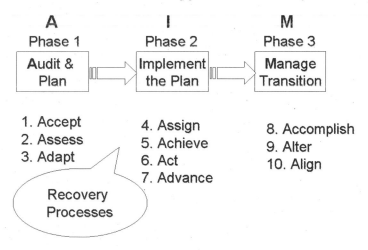

Project Recovery Process
AIM Methodology for Recovery

A	I	M
Phase 1	Phase 2	Phase 3
Audit & Plan	Implement the Plan	Manage Transition

1. Accept	4. Assign	8. Accomplish
2. Assess	5. Achieve	9. Alter
3. Adapt	6. Act	10. Align
	7. Advance	

Recovery Processes

© Dhanu Kothari & Romeo Mitchell 2007

35

Taken together, the three phases form the basis of the **AIM©**
Methodology for Project Recovery as shown in Figure 4-B. Each
one of the phases in turn consists of a number of processes
which are described later.

The AIM Recovery Methodology

Phase 1   Audit and Plan (A)

The objective of this phase is to determine the chances of the
project's survival, identify appropriate strategies and develop a
preliminary action plan. It involves fact-finding and diagnosing the
scope and severity of the project's problems.

Once major problems and opportunities are identified, the
Recovery Manager develops a strategic plan with specific goals
and detailed functional actions. This plan must then be sold to all
key parties in the company, including the management team,
stakeholders and the project team.

This phase focuses on planning for recovery and it consists of
three processes: **Accept, Assess and Adapt.**

A1 - Accept

This refers to an acknowledgement by the sponsors that the
project is in trouble. It involves getting them to accept the situation
if they are in denial. One of the major reasons why a project
recovery fails is that the need for recovery is not recognized until
it is too late.

A2 - Assess

The situation is assessed by reviewing available documentation,
conducting interviews and completing fact gathering relative to
the best practices for managing successful projects. These
include a description business case, project charter, statement of
work, scope definition, detailed schedule, communication plan,
risk management, project organization, roles and responsibilities,
status reports, minutes of meetings and change requests.

A3 - Adapt

A course of action is planned and developed for implementing the recovery. It starts with understanding changes to the original plan, adapting it and restructuring it for purposes of recovery. It includes a revised Project Charter (which is different from a Recovery Charter), an implementation roadmap, a detailed schedule, management commitment for required resources, and a list of project deliverables. It may also include an Emergency Action Plan designed to stop the bleeding on the project right away.

Phase 2   Implement the Plan (I)

The objectives of this phase are to execute the project plan by following standard project management principles and practices. It covers all of the basic Project Management responsibilities associated with getting work done. Key steps in this phase are to:

- Delegate and assign responsibilities to team members, and get their commitments

- Ensure that associated milestones and deliverables are clearly communicated and understood by the team, and

- Advance the project through communications, coordination and control.

The major processes associated with the Implement phase are: **Assign, Achieve, Act and Advance.**

A4 - Assign

Steps are designed to ensure effective delegation of work. It starts with a recovery kick-off meeting with the project team to review the updated Project Charter and ensures that the team understands how the project will be managed till its closure. It sets ground rules and processes for managing the project with best practices, and requires that every work package has designated individuals who are responsible for accepting, approving, defining and delivering it.

A5 - Achieve

Targets are set based on Specifc, Measurable, Achievable, Realistic and Target-driven (SMART) objectives. The road to recovery consists of intermediate objectives that must be clearly defined with respect to their success criteria and deliverables.

A6 - Act

Practices, tools and techniques are implemented for instituting a consistent and predictable process of problem solving and decision making. A successful recovery depends on consultative selling and getting the "buy-in" of stakeholders through discussions, facilitations and negotiations. This process addresses the relationship between the process of decision making and the action of decision taking.

A7 - Advance

Project objectives are continually upheld and it ensured that the project team is held together by a common purpose. As with many other projects, the Recovery Manager acts as a salesperson and an evangelist for the project. This is crucial to ensure the team stays committed to project goals. This process includes all the vehicles for project communication that are required to advance the project towards its completion.

Phase 3   Manage the Transition (M)

The major processes in the transition phase focus on stabilizing and ensuring an orderly transfer of project to the Project Manager. Stabilization is confirmed when the recovery project is following the recommended policies, processes and procedures on a regular basis, they are working successfully and are fully accepted by its stakeholders.

At this point, the Recovery Manager transfers the responsibility to the ongoing Project Manager and completes the transition. Transition is also associated with building the foundation for Program Governance leading to a Program Management Office (PMO), Program Portfolio Management (PPM) and continuous improvement in the organization.

The processes associated with the transition phase are: **Accomplish, Alter, Align**

A8 - Accomplish

Increased confidence on the part of the project team accomplishes stability. Overall stakeholder satisfaction regarding timeliness and quality of deliverables, and management support and commitment steadies the project. The atmosphere of malaise and mistrust is replaced by confidence and credibility, and the Recovery Manager is ready to move on.

A9 - Alter

A change is made in the direction of the project through effective coaching and transition to the Project Manager. The coaching cycle begins early in the recovery project and it deals with building trust, gaining commitment and developing the Project Manager's skills. It includes establishing a process for managing all aspects of the project and stabilizing the project through a common understanding of its future direction with all stakeholders.

A10 - Align

The organizational structure, discipline and management processes for on-going execution of future projects are put onto alignment. It encompasses the concepts of Program Governance, Program Portfolio Management, standardized methodologies and processes for achieving continuous improvement.

The following table illustrates the flow of major activities in the AIM Methodology.

The AIM Methodology – Major Activities

Quick Scans	Phase 1 Audit and Plan (A)	Phase 2 Implement the Plan (I)	Phase 3 Manage the Transition (M)
▫ Conduct Initial Quick Scan	▫ Conduct Compliance Quick Scans	▫ Deliver Quick Wins as per the Inch-Stone Plan	▫ Stabilize project environment
▫ Understand the environment	▫ Conduct Project Health-Check	▫ Follow Best Practices for Project Mgt.	▫ Introduce mgt. of change
▫ Ensure recovery is viable	▫ "Deep Dive" into specific areas	▫ Introduce std. & consistent processes	▫ Transfer responsibility to ongoing Project Manager
▫ Confirm mgt. commitment	▫ Analyze and evaluate options	▫ Make progress visible	
▫ Establish win conditions for recovery	▫ Confirm Recovery Objectives	▫ Build open & honest comm.	▫ Conduct "Lessons Learned"
▫ Develop a Recovery Charter	▫ Get stakeholder acceptance	▫ Coach PM and Project Team	
	▫ Prepare a Recovery Plan	▫ Revise/ Project Charter	▫ Promote Program Governance
	▫ Include a granular "Inch-stone" plan	▫ Develop new baseline	

Ground Rules for Recovery

In addition to the methodology and processes, Recovery Managers follow certain ground rules to stay focused on the project and recovery objectives. The ground rules are applicable regardless of the complexity, scope and technology of the project.

AIMing for Recovery - Ground Rules

- Avoid discussion of project history
- Understand the "As Is" state and expectations for the "To Be" state
- Focus on business needs, objectives and strategic alignment
- Scrutinize project requirements in relation to business needs
- Validate cost justification for each requirement

- Focus the discussion on "Process" instead of "People" issues
- Review & redefine project organization, roles and responsibilities
- Consider design of alternatives and new solutions
- Get agreement on the objectives of recovery and success criteria
- Conduct project health check; Assess the situation
- Do problem analysis to understand the root causes
- Fix the project bleeding right away and get a recovery plan first
- Plan the recovery effort as if it were a new project
- Consider the time & effort required to implement management of change
- Focus on Communications, Change control, Risk mg. and Personnel issues
- Don't shy away from bad news. Foster open and honest communication
- Focus on the project. Do not attempt to solve organizational or systemic problems
- Lead by example. Follow the "Show-Do" model. Coach the project manager and the project team.

AIMing for Recovery

The AIM Methodology along with its three phases and ten processes and ground rules for recovery is the foundation of the A10© Model for Project Recovery as shown in Figure 4-C.

Figure 4-C

Project Recovery - The A^{10} Model©

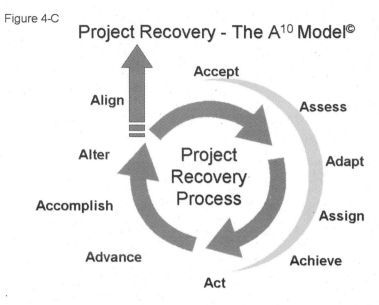

© Dhanu Kothari & Romeo Mitchell 2007

Chapters 5-14 address details of the A10 processes as listed below:

A1   **Accept** ... the Fact

A2   **Assess** ... the Project

A3   **Adapt** ... Objectives to Business Needs

A4   **Assign** ... Responsibilities and Delegate

A5   **Achieve** ... Goals by Setting Targets

A6   **Act** ... Consistently and Decisively

A7   **Advance** ... the Project through Communications

A8   **Accomplish** ... Stability for Turnover

A9   **Alter** ... Direction through Transition

A10   **Align** ... Processes for On-going Execution

42

05   a1 - accept the fact

Project Recovery - The A^{10} Model©

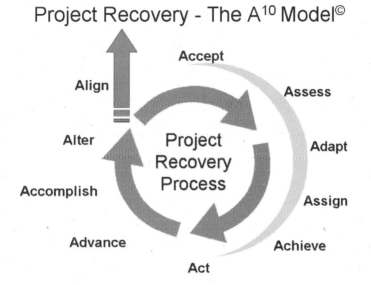

The greatest obstacle to project recovery is individual or organizational resistance to accepting that the project is in trouble. Often, the Recovery Manager is brought in because one of the senior executives is concerned about the issues or progress of the project, but cannot get others to even acknowledge that there is a serious issue. This can happen due to many reasons.

How Organizations Work

Organizations are prone to operate with a psychology of denial until it is too late to recover from a troubled or a potentially disastrous situation. There is resistance to recognizing the fact that a potential risk is imminent or that it has happened.

Nobody wishes to acknowledge that the originally proposed solution, as it was deigned, doesn't work. There are different players, perceptions and political considerations that come into the picture, and they have many influences on the project and its course. There are personal and cultural rivalries that filter all the way from top management to individual project teams. Finally, there is always someone else to blame – clients who don't know what they want, stakeholders who are uncooperative, and team members who are not skilled.

In these situations, the overall game plan is focussed on "containment" rather than recovery, resulting in a concerted effort to "Delay, Diminish and Downplay" the bad news about the status of a project.

Taken to its extreme, it results in knee-jerk reactions, manipulation of data, misrepresentation of facts and organizational hubris practiced at various levels in the organization - sometimes deliberately, often unknowingly and mostly driven by a psychology of denial.

Psychology of Denial

The psychology of denial is rooted in a resistance to accept reality. It is evident when management and team members indulge in practicing the following patterns of behaviour. Figure 5 illustrates the environment that leads to the psychology of denial.

- "Shoot the messenger" attitude

This is based on a culture of fear and thrives on management practices that are reluctant to discuss challenging and difficult issues facing a project. "Just get it done or else ..." is the implied threat to the individual who is waving the red flag and asking for help.

- Failure to speak up

It is the very nature of projects that problems arise and unexpected things happen. It is expected that team members openly deliberate and discuss project issues, options and risks to chart a proper course of action. When they do not speak up, or refrain from doing so for fear of "sticking one's neck out", then the project is headed towards a rathole.

From a recovery perspective, it is not a problem that we have problems on the project. It is, however, a serious problem when we don't talk about them openly or prevent their discussion.

- Filtering of information

  Organizations are wired to filter information as it travels up the management chain and make things appear optimistic & positive. Nobody wants to be the bearer of bad news, and it can be twisted and manipulated in many ways to make it look good. It also creates the impression that the individual feeding the information is in full control of the situation.

- Organization culture

  Some organizations develop a culture typified by "damn the torpedoes; full speed ahead" thinking. The target date has been decided; the President put a stake in the ground; there is no turning back - regardless of risks and consequences - so goes the thinking that leaves no room for a reality check.

Figure 5

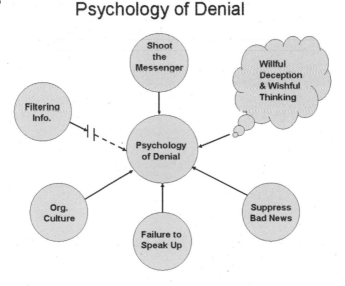

Psychology of Denial

© Dhanu Kothari & Romeo Mitchell 2007

- Suppression of bad news

  The name of the game is to "Delay, diminish or downplay" the bad news as long as one can, while hoping that it will simply go away or be overtaken by something else that is hopefully positive. In this scenario, managing the client's expectations, the key criteria for a successful project, turns itself into a public relations exercise for "Managing perceptions".

"Wilful deception" and "Wishful thinking" are the two outcomes of the psychology of denial. One fosters the ostrich-like mentality of burying one's head in the sand, and the other results in inaction and a general sense of malaise in the project team. Neither of them is helpful towards managing a successful project.

The Recovery Manager is often expected to deal with this mentality, establish as much objectivity about the project as possible, and help stakeholders to accept the situation. Without acceptance, any talk of recovery is redundant.

Getting Stakeholder Acceptance

How does one get the stakeholders to accept that a project is in trouble? First, you look for the symptoms, gather facts, do a diagnosis and then present the evidence of the project's troubled state. Questions related to the following points are helpful towards getting a quick understanding of the situation:

- Project Fundamentals: Definition of project scope, plans, risks and schedules based on Specific, Measurable, Achievable, Realistic and Target-driven objectives (SMART)

- Project Drivers: The dominant factors and dependencies that influence the direction of the project (e.g. Technology, Organization, Processes etc.); Completion and Success Criteria

- Project Purpose: Business need that is being addressed and strategic importance of the project; Business value associated with the project.

- Roles and Responsibilities: Specific names associated with the roles of key stakeholders including the Project Manager, Project Sponsor and Client Manager, and a clear understanding of their responsibilities

- Team Morale: The overall feeling of confidence and team morale reflected in the language surrounding the project (e.g. "It's a mess"; "Wouldn't touch it with a ten foot pole"; "I am outta here" etc.) The project is in trouble when the language of the team hides reality and becomes ambiguous, coded, terse or vague.

These points form the basis of a simple list of "Acid Test Questions" that can be asked to help diagnose the troubled state of a project. Using the answers to these questions, the Recovery Manager follows the following five steps to gain stakeholders' acceptance.

1. Review project background and Identify the "Quick indicators" of a troubled state:

   - Measurable Criteria - Variations re Actual, Budget, Deliverables, Signoffs, Earned Value (EV), Estimate to Complete (ETC)
   - Variable Factors - Lack of Project Documentation, Risk Plans
   - Human Factors - Lack of Management Support, Sponsorship, Client Participation, Organizational Readiness
   - Other Constraints- Contractual, Legal

2. Examine team confidence and morale as indicated by lack of purpose, level of trust, feeling of burnout, lack of confidence, trust in leadership and intensity of client interaction.

3. Identify risks and consequences of continuing with the current state.

4. Identify stakeholders who are in denial/resistance; Set up one-on-one interviews with those that are most at risk; Review status and potential consequences; Obtain feedback on their perspectives.

5. Build on the support of key stakeholders and present to management.

Acceptance Indicators

How does one know that the project stakeholders are open to accepting reality?

There are several indicators starting with a growing belief by stakeholders in the "Quick Indicators" and objectivity. It is followed by an acknowledgement of symptoms confirming that things are not well with the project. They begin to demonstrate an open mindset based on willingness to listen and they participate in active listening.

The discussion moves away from a "Blame Game" or a "Witch Hunt" to alternatives for resolving and moving forward. Finally, there is a sense of urgency to act and do the right thing to recover the project.

The Project Recovery Manager plays an important role in getting the stakeholders to accept the situation and in building a positive attitude towards moving forward with a detailed assessment. Acceptance leads to Assessment - the next step in the A10 Recovery Methodology.

Tools and Techniques for Gaining Acceptance

- Quick Scans
- Project Review and Snapshot
- Stakeholder Analysis Matrix
- Client/Stakeholder Satisfaction Survey
- One on one meetings for gathering data and information
- Project documentation review for existence and type

06

a2 – assess the situation

Project Recovery - The A^{10} Model©

The main objectives of the assessment process are to determine the current state of the project and to recommend a course of action, based on the rationale for project recovery or cancellation. In the case of recovery, the detailed assessment identifies the changes required in order to regain control of the project.

Such changes may be required in people, the product, processes or tools that are associated with the project. Sometimes it is people that need changing. The assessment also validates the assumptions, business need and cost justification for the project, and it lays the foundation for planning the recovery.

As part of the assessment, the assessor reviews available documentation, conducts interviews and evaluates the overall state of the project relative to the best practices for managing successful projects. The best practices include an approved business case, a project charter, a statement of work, scope definition, detailed schedule, communication plan, risk management, project organization, roles and responsibilities, status reports, minutes of meetings and change requests. It also includes an evaluation of all open items along with an estimate of work needed to close them.

The assessment process consists of five major activities:

1. Performing a Health Check
2. Building an Assessment Plan
3. Conducting "Deep Dives" for focused investigations
4. Performing a Detailed Assessment
5. Building a Recovery Roadmap

Activity 1 - Perform Project Health Check

The first activity in the Assessment process is the Project Health Check, which is used as a tool for providing valuable feedback on the use and effectiveness of project planning, quality, and delivery throughout the organization.

In addition to learning about the project's objectives, deliverables and outcomes, the Health Check also provides insight into the business context, people, politics, relationships and trade-offs involved in the project. It helps to identify project strengths and weaknesses, and key areas that need to be addressed to achieve recovery or improvements.

The major components of Health Check are:

- Health Check Plan: Consisting of scope, roles, responsibilities and schedule

- Inputs to Health Check: Consisting of Health Check questionnaire, evaluation criteria, project documents, risk profile and summary of interviews

- Variance Analysis: Consisting of a review of baselines for cost, schedule, performance and variances with respect to each, existence of a technical solution; clarity of scope, changes to the project, and ongoing developments that contribute to progress or act as inhibitors

- Health Check Report: Consisting of project strengths, areas for improvement, recommendations and action items

The Health Check Plan formalizes the authority and process for conducting the Health Check. With the exception of very complex projects, a short document outlining its purpose, expectations from participants, expected outcomes and confirmation of management support is sufficient. The Plan, however, must be in place to give legitimacy to and gain acceptance of the Health Check.

Health Check Questionnaire

The basis for developing the Health Check Questionnaire is the "Ten Best Practices" listed in Figure 6-A The following checklist is suggested for developing a questionnaire and evaluating the health of a project by simply checking 1 for "Yes" or 0 for "No" for each statement.

Figure 6-A

Recovery Health Check - Best Practices
Ref. "Rainbows & Ratholes: Best practices for Managing Successful Projects"

1. Business Case & Project Charter
2. Project Organization Chart
3. Work Breakdown Structure
4. Dependency Chart, Critical Path, Major Milestones, Work Packages & Deliverables
5. RACI/RAM Chart (Resp. Assignment)
6. Risk Assessment & Risk Plan
7. Financial Plan with the Six Measures
8. Project Change Control
9. Status Reports, Issues & Escalations
10. Team Interaction and Team Morale

© Dhanu Kothari & Romeo Mitchell 2007

The statements are designed to bring out the existence or non-existence of fundamental best practices for managing successful projects. The final score out of the total of 50 will provide a firm indication of the current state of the project - the lower the score, the higher is the need for recovery.

Business Case & Project Charter

☐ There is an approved business case based on project benefits, return on investment (ROI) and business value

☐ A Project Charter with approved budgets, costs and risks is signed off by the Project Sponsor, Key Stakeholders and Management Committee

☐ The project is aligned with business needs, objectives, priorities and strategies of the organization

☐ The Project Charter is approved by the Project Sponsor and key stakeholders

☐ Business needs for undertaking the project are relevant and applicable

Project Organization

☐ Roles, responsibilities and accountabilities are clearly defined and accepted

☐ Specific individuals, with names and titles, are identified with the critical roles of Project Manager, Client Manager, Project Sponsor, Project Engineer etc.

☐ Key stakeholders - individuals or organizations who are impacted by, or have an interest in the outcome of the project, are identified and actively involved in the project.

☐ The Project Sponsor demonstrates commitment to the project through active policy leadership, business direction, ownership, resolution and support as required... beyond being merely a figure-head!

- ☐ The Project Manager accepts responsibility for the strategic and tactical success or failure of the project, and manages all aspects including scope, cost, schedule, resources, risk, communication, procurement, quality and the overall integration of people, process and technology components of the project

Work Breakdown Structure

- ☐ A Work Breakdown Structure (WBS) of the project listing its components, sub-components and work packages is available

- ☐ The WBS was prepared in consultation with the client and key stakeholders, and there is a common understanding of the deliverables among all participants

- ☐ Each work package has a completion criteria and a list of deliverables leading to the overall success criteria for the project

- ☐ Requirements can be traced back to business need, rationale, measurement, completion criteria and measure of success

- ☐ Cost, schedule and productivity measures can be traced back to the Work Breakdown Structure

Dependency Chart & Critical Path

- ☐ Intermediate milestones and associated deliverables are clearly defined

- ☐ The critical path is identified and communicated to the project team

- ☐ Key personal accountabilities including who, when, what etc. are specified

- ☐ Information on float for activities and resources is available to help with decision making and deployment in emergencies

- [ ] There are contingency plans to work around if the critical path is in jeopardy

RACI or RAM Chart (Responsibility Assignment Matrix)

- [ ] Adequate resources are assigned to the project as per the project plan

- [ ] All members of the project team have the required competencies, skills and training

- [ ] A matrix outlining work packages, deliverables, responsibilities and approvals exists

- [ ] Project team members believe that assigned targets are realistic and achievable

- [ ] An up to date record of completed, in-process and outstanding work packages and assignments is available

Risk Assessment & Risk Plan

- [ ] An up to date Risk Management Plan outlining major risks to the project is available

- [ ] The risk plan identifies major risks associated with Technology, Implementation, Management and Organizational aspects of the project

- [ ] Management is aware of the risks associated with the project and has approved the Risk Management Plan

- [ ] Funding for executing the Risk Plan is in place in the event of risk occurrence

- [ ] The risks are consistent with the business strategies and goals

Financial Plan with Six Measures

- [ ] The project is approved and fully funded

- ☐ There is a detailed cost plan for the project and a summary cost plan to the end

- ☐ Up to date data on six financial measures (e.g. actuals, budgets, cumulative values, earned value analysis, estimate to complete and variances) is available

- ☐ Project cash flow data is up to date and readily available

- ☐ Costs and approvals associated with project changes, procurements and sub-contractor activities are verifiable

Project Change Control

- ☐ There is a standard Change Control process and it is used consistently

- ☐ Documentation exists to validate that Change Requests are recorded, evaluated, approved and implemented

- ☐ The cost, frequency and number of changes requested in relation to the overall project plan and deliverables are manageable

- ☐ The changes are perceived as adding value to the project rather than acting as inhibitors to progress

- ☐ There is a manual or an automated tool that provides an integrated view of the impact and inter-relationships of the changes (e.g. configuration management)

Status Reports, Issues & Escalations

- ☐ Weekly status reports, minutes of meetings, issues and escalations are documented and communicated on a timely basis

- ☐ Status reports accurately reflect the state of the project including accomplishments to date, planned activities, potential problems, project challenges, management escalations and recommended actions

☐ A communication matrix outlining a list of recipients and communication documents for information distribution exists

☐ A process for timely escalation and resolution of issues is documented and followed

☐ There is an overall acceptance that project communication is informative, meaningful, relevant and useful.

Team Interaction and Morale

☐ Team members have confidence and a sense of common purpose regarding the project

☐ There is a culture of cooperation and trust, and there is positive interaction among team members

☐ Discussions regarding project issues are held in an open manner without fear or threat of reprisals

☐ The team is cohesive and team members enjoy meeting the project challenge

☐ The client is satisfied with the quality of deliverables and interaction with the project team

Questionnaire Assessment

Check the score by counting "Yes" responses to the questions and refer to the guideline below for a quick appraisal of the state of the troubled project and recommended actions.

Score	Conclusion	Action
1-10	Rationale or justification for doing the project is questionable	Terminate Project
11-20	Implement basic Project Management processes and Re-plan	Major Recovery
21-30	Identify critical needs & requirements; Re-scope and deliver	Normal Recovery
31-40	Focus on stakeholder relationships & managing expectations	Minor Recovery
41+	Deliver as planned; Sell business value; Make it visible	Follow the Plan

Activity 2 - Build an Assessment Plan

The next step is to build an Assessment Plan which includes drilling down the details and identifying the following for the plan: Assessment objectives, Work breakdown structure for conducting the assessment, Resources for assessment, Risk and problem management, Schedule, Tools for each task, List of deliverables, War room needs, and Kickoff meeting details. The effort for this activity will vary based on results of the Health Check and the specific areas that will be assessed.

Based on the questionnaire, the plan should include a review of the following:

- Project charter and objectives
- Estimated cost and schedule
- Business needs and Requirements
- Scope definition and Statement of work
- Solution architecture and technical design
- Project plans and status reports
- Project deliverables and Completion Criteria
- Internal and external agreements
- Project organization, roles and responsibilities
- Project Workbook and related documentation

A formal sign-off may be required depending upon the complexity, size and scope of the assessment.

Activity 3 - Conduct "Deep Dives"

The purpose of the "Deep Dive" is two-fold: First, to get a quick grasp of the situation with respect to specific issues in the project as outlined in the Health Check, and second, to appraise everyone on the purpose and process of the assessment.

During this activity, the Recovery Manager builds a rapport with stakeholders, gains their confidence, explains the process and sets their expectations.

The "Deep Dive" sets the stage for conducting assessments in the following areas as required:

- Project Priority, Complexity & Criticality
- Project Organization & Players
- Client's Interest & Expectations
- Team Morale & Confidence
- Solution & Alternatives

News regarding an upcoming assessment generates a high level of apprehension and concern among all participants, and in particular, among the project team members. Many personalities and egos are involved in the project, and people are unwilling to participate in the assessment due to its possible implications regarding their earlier decisions and judgements.

The "Deep Dive" sets the stage for everybody's cooperation in the detailed assessment by assuring them that its main purpose is to recover the project and not to conduct a "witch hunt".

Activity 4 – Perform a Detailed Assessment

The main objectives of this part of the assessment phase are to determine the current status of the project, and identify major threats, opportunities, and problems confronting it. Major activities include Requirements Analysis, Project Organization Assessment, Risk and Complexity Analysis, SWOT Analysis and Root Cause Analysis.

The objective of the Requirements Analysis is to validate the requirements and identify the most critical ones for recovery based on the following seven crucial questions:

- What is the Business Need?
- What are the Requirements that fulfill the Need?
- What is the Rationale for the Requirement?
- How will you measure it?
- How will you know when the Requirement is met?
- How does this Requirement relate to other Requirements?
- What is the priority and how important is it?

The purpose of Project Organization Assessment is to identify situations with conflicting, missing or overlapping roles and responsibilities so that they can be resolved for the purpose of executing the recovery and ongoing management of the project.

Risk Analysis identifies major risks as they relate to technology, implementation, management and organizational aspects of the project, and develops a risk profile to assist with recovery decisions.

Complexity analysis provides a measure of the difficulty in integrating various constraints, interfaces and technologies required for the solution. The SWOT analysis focuses on the strengths, weaknesses, opportunities and threats related to the possibility of a recovery.

Finally, the Root Cause Analysis (RCA) helps towards understanding the most likely causes that contributed to a troubled state of the project, and identifying those that can be addressed within the scope of the recovery.

An example of RCA showing the most likely root causes of a troubled project is provided in Figure 6-B.

Figure 6-B

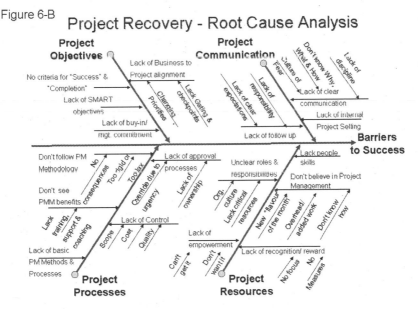

Project Recovery - Root Cause Analysis

© Dhanu Kothari & Romeo Mitchell 2007

Completing the Assessment

The outcome of the Assessment process is a report and recommendations that are presented to the assessment sponsor for decision making regarding recovery or termination of the project. The assessment should be treated as a short project, consisting of a standard project lifecycle: concept, development, execution, and finish or closeout. The sponsor's approval of the assessment and its recommendations sets the stage for the next process in the Recovery Cycle which is planning for recovery – Adapt project outcome to business needs.

Activity 5 - Building the Recovery Plan

The Recovery Plan has two components. First, it addresses the areas that will be under review and refinement by the Recovery Manager as required, such as Project Charter, Business Case and WBS etc. Second, it outlines the project areas that will be managed by the Project Manager as part of ongoing project activities during the recovery period, depending on the scope and complexity of recovery.

Preparing the Roadmap

The recovery roadmap consists of four stages: (1) Develop a Dependency Diagram (2) Understand the Critical Path (3) Finalize the Project Schedule (4) Develop an Inch-Stone Plan

The first stage consists of analysis, and it gives us an understanding of what and how the work should be performed. The second stage consists of synthesis, and it tells us what is driving the duration and cost of the project. The third stage helps us to "put a stake in the ground" based on available resources and other constraints, and finalize the roadmap and the schedule. Finally, the fourth stage provides the means to generate confidence and credibility by ensuring "quick wins" and demonstrable progress in regaining control of the project.

- *Stage 1 - Develop a Dependency Diagram*

This starts with a one page overview of major milestones and a list of the major activities associated with each milestone. A dependency diagram is developed based on activity constraints, dependencies and relationships. The diagram is a visual model of the flow of project work that represents activities in logical order and sequence. An example of a dependency diagram with an implementation roadmap for a complex recovery is shown in Chapter 9: Achieve Goals by Setting Realistic Targets.

- *Stage 2 - Understand the Critical Path*

It consists of breaking down the major activities into smaller work pieces - approx. of 1 week duration or less. The ground rules for estimating are followed and the Critical Path is identified. Reasonable assumptions are made for deriving estimates and they are documented. Focus is placed on activities on the critical path

- *Stage 3 - Finalize the Schedule*

First, a schedule-constrained plan is prepared and then modified based on resource availability constraints. Alternatives to expedite, accelerate, modify or sequence activities with the objective of reducing the overall duration are considered through an iterative process. The final schedule reflects consensus on tradeoffs, and it is kept aggressive but achievable.

- *Stage 4 - Develop an "Inch-Stone" Plan*

A rolling Inch-Stone plan covering the first 2-3 weeks of recovery is developed. It consists of a frequent, and often daily, list of smaller milestones and deliverables that are designed to re-establish confidence in the recovery. The initial Inch-Stone plan is purposely designed to facilitate micro-management.

Tools/Techniques for Assessment

- Project Health Check
- Root Cause Analysis - Cause and Effect Diagram
- Questionnaire based on Ten Best Practices
- Pre-assessment Organization Model
- Requirements Assessment Tool

07 a3 - adapt project outcome to business needs

Project Recovery - The A^{10} Model©

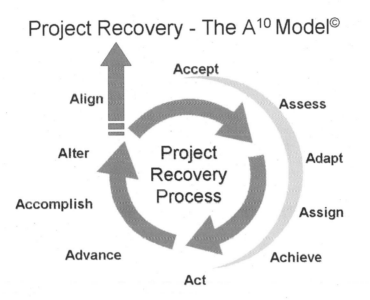

The third process in the recovery cycle is "Adapt". Its objective is to assess business needs, reset project objectives and re-draw project plans subject to what can be realistically achieved as part of recovery.

The process includes questioning and challenging project fundamentals based on the results of assessment, however, the objective is to evolve the project to a stable state, not to conduct a witch-hunt. The focus of this process is on moving forward rather than discussing project history and past events.

During this process, the Recovery Manager should be highly sensitive to people's emotions, perceptions and reactions, since its success depends on a number of trade-offs in relation to the original project objectives and expectations.

Stakeholders need to be made aware of what can be fixed, what cannot be fixed and the risks involved in the planned recovery. Team members need to understand, and commit themselves to, the objectives of recovery as set out in the Recovery Plan. There are no ready-made formulas, and there is no silver bullet solution.

Recovery Objectives

A recovery can only be successful if it is accomplished in the context of the project objectives that satisfy a business or organizational need. This is accomplished through a recovery plan that has a "buy-in" from key participants. The plan may hinge on various options such as scaling down the scope, redesigning the solution or renegotiating the terms for the project.

The primary focus of recovery is on:

- Reestablishing stakeholder confidence in the project
- Rebuilding the project team
- Resolving project issues
- Producing an achievable schedule
- Negotiating and updating to realistic project baselines

Executing the Recovery Plan begins with the refinement and updating of the Project Charter which outlines the purpose of the project, roles and responsibilities, high level resource commitments, target dates, risks and funding.

Refining the Project Charter for Recovery

A Project Charter is the crucial link between business strategy and project goals. It is an implicit recognition of the need for and a commitment to the project, by senior management. It validates the project's alignment with business needs that arise from an organization's strategies and goals - an increase in revenue, an improvement in customer service, a reduction in costs, a gain in market share etc.

Each business goal, in turn, spawns a number of related projects designed to contribute to it. For each project, there is a list of project objectives which form the basis for the project scope for the work to be performed.

The vast majority of decisions relating to projects are subjected to a complex process of communication, often leading to a troubled state: Strategies leading to goals, goals leading to projects, projects leading to objectives, and finally, objectives leading to project scope.

By the time one is assigned to the project, it has gone through several levels of assumptions, communication, filtering, interpretations, spin and translations. Bottom line ... much is lost in the communication.

That is the nature of organizations, and also one of the primary causes for troubled projects. Even under the best of circumstances, assuming 90% integrity in communications, the project scope is only 70% aligned with the business goals at the start of the project!

The potential for misalignment exists at the same time when a project is approved, and it can easily degenerate into a troubled project if it is not monitored carefully. Therefore, the first priority in planning for recovery is to ensure ongoing project to business alignment with the following six steps:

Ensuring the Project to Business Alignment - The Six Steps

1. Ask questions from a management perspective and get answers from as many sources as you can. Lack of answers or significantly different answers indicate a lack of management support and commitment. Quite often, it is a matter of wide ranging and divergent expectations where people view the same project differently.

2. Understand how the project is aligned with the organization's business strategies and goals. The Recovery Manager ought to know about the client's business, organization culture, business goals and their relationship with the project.

3. Sell the recovery. The recovery, just like the project, is going to affect people, processes, roles and scope of their jobs. People are afraid of change and will resist it. The success of recovery

depends on getting everyone's buy-in and enthusiastic participation in the project.

4. Articulate benefits of recovery from a business perspective. How will the recovery benefit the organization, the customer and the end user? Elevate the discussion from technical jargon to a higher plane that the client can understand.

5. Validate the project-business alignment and its objectives throughout the life cycle of the project. The project scope that was agreed to at the beginning may not be valid any more since organizations, strategies and management priorities are always changing.

6. Subject the project objectives through the SMART lens. Are they Specific? Are they Measurable? Are they Achievable? Are they Realistic? And finally, are they Target-driven? Does the scope have an exit strategy? How do you know when you are done?

At this point, the project objectives are revalidated, adjusted and, if necessary, realigned to satisfy the business as well as recovery objectives. The project scoping and re-baselining work is started with the development of a Work Breakdown Structure (WBS).

Creating and Refining the WBS

The proven technique for scoping a project is known as the Work Breakdown Structure (WBS). It is achieved through a thought process that breaks down a project into many components to such levels of clarity and granularity that each component can be assigned to a team member and treated as a responsible unit.

The Recovery Manager is experienced in the use of various approaches and models for developing a WBS, and chooses the right one based on how best to organize, slice and manage the recovery. The WBS is prepared with involvement of the client, the project team and specialists who know the subject matter in this process. Involvement leads to commitment, giving people a sense of ownership and responsibility.

The end result of the WBS process is a manageable and controllable project environment that allows the Project Manager to focus on people and not on individual tasks. The WBS provides a solid foundation for baselining the schedule. That is why successful Recovery Managers believe that if you don't have the WBS, then all you are working with is "BS"!

Adjusting the Schedule for the New Baseline

The adjusted baseline schedule is a result of negotiation with, and commitments from various stakeholders, based on realistic and achievable goals, and subject to the constraints of project funding, resources and time. In the case of recovery, the original project schedule and cost have to re-baselined.

The following guidelines as illustrated in Figure 7-A are suggested for developing the baseline schedule:

1. Establish the Business Need (Strategy, Goals and Objectives) - This should indicate the reason for doing the project, the goals and objectives of the project.

2. Prepare a Statement of Work (SOW) - The basis for the SOW is a good requirement definition. The requirements for the project are stated in simple, clear, unambiguous terms and they are independent of the technology that will be used in the solution.

3. Define the high level solution - This includes a recommended solution approach, components of the solution, internal or external sources for acquiring components, and a Request for Proposal (RFP) for the components to be sub-contracted.

4. Plan the work and activities to accomplish the project - This includes project definition, Work Breakdown Structure (WBS), project components, Work Packages and Activities.

5. Define activities - List activities for each work package and identify the sequence, dependencies and deliverables for each activity and dependencies.

6. Establish major milestones - Milestones are points or events in time. Select milestones at 2-3 week intervals that represent significant progress and achievement on the project.

Figure 7-A

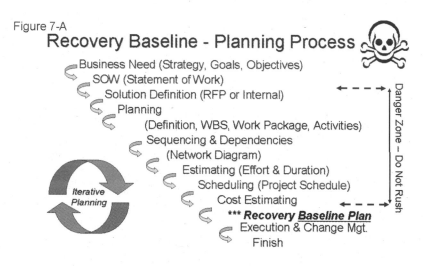

Recovery Baseline - Planning Process

Business Need (Strategy, Goals, Objectives)
SOW (Statement of Work)
Solution Definition (RFP or Internal)
Planning
(Definition, WBS, Work Package, Activities)
Sequencing & Dependencies
(Network Diagram)
Estimating (Effort & Duration)
Scheduling (Project Schedule)
Cost Estimating
*** Recovery Baseline Plan
Execution & Change Mgt.
Finish

Iterative Planning

Danger Zone – Do Not Rush

Follow the Process to "Baseline" the Project, then
Use automated PM tools to execute the baseline plan

© Dhanu Kothari & Romeo Mitchell 2007

7. Prepare a dependency diagram - List, organize and display major activities associated with each milestone. Prepare a visual model of how the project will be done.

8. Estimate effort and duration - Make reasonable assumptions for timing, availability and quantity of resources, technology and equipment. Break down activities into durations of 1 week or less, if necessary.

9. Develop the schedule - This will require iterative planning subject to time, resource and budget constraints. It includes a review of alternative strategies for fast tracking the project.

10. Finalize the Baseline schedule - Select a strategy that makes the best sense for the organization and the client, and develop the schedule based on available and committed

resources. Transfer the schedule to an electronic project scheduling tool.

Evolving Towards a New Baseline

The final output of the "Adapt" process is a Project Workbook that includes a comprehensive baseline plan for the recovery project. The workbook consists of a series of planning documents collectively known as the Implementation or Baseline Plan, and a set of working documents required for operational and reference purposes.

The working documents include :

- Supporting and technical documentation such as Requirements Definition, Statement of Work, Design Specifications, Solution Design or Architecture, Manufacturing or Development Specifications, Test Strategies, Test Results, Training Guides and Support and Maintenance documentation

- Project Control documentation such as Work Assignments, weekly Status Reports, Minutes of Meetings, Escalations to Management, Outstanding Issues Log, Sign-offs and Completion Reports.

The Project Workbook is the primary vehicle to ensure that the project team members have a common, consistent and clear understanding of the project, the related documentation and its progress as shown In Figure 7-B.

Building the Revised Project Plan

The revised Project Plan ensures that all the necessary aspects of planning are addressed:

☐ *Project Goals, Objectives and Scope*

The revised statement of goals, objectives and scope establishes a common understanding of the business purpose and provides justification for the project. It clearly identifies the project sponsor, project manager, client manager, funding sources, budgetary considerations and success criteria.

☐ *Project Organization*

The Project Organization clearly defines the roles and responsibilities of the individuals assigned to the project including specific names associated with the roles of Project Sponsor, Manager and Client Acceptor.

☐ *Work Breakdown Structure*

The first step in breaking down the project into manageable and assignable tasks in the form of a "family tree" is the Work Breakdown Structure. It forces the project team to define "what" before the "how". It establishes the scope baseline and provides the basis for measuring and reporting scope performance.

☐ *Major Milestones*

Major milestones define key events in the project life cycle and provide the means to assess whether a project is on target. Associated with each milestone are major tasks and activities which must be 100% completed for achieving the milestone.

Figure 7-B

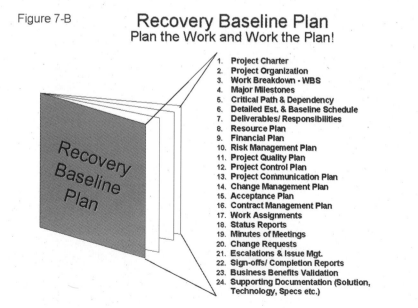

Recovery Baseline Plan
Plan the Work and Work the Plan!

1. Project Charter
2. Project Organization
3. Work Breakdown - WBS
4. Major Milestones
5. Critical Path & Dependency
6. Detailed Est. & Baseline Schedule
7. Deliverables/ Responsibilities
8. Resource Plan
9. Financial Plan
10. Risk Management Plan
11. Project Quality Plan
12. Project Control Plan
13. Project Communication Plan
14. Change Management Plan
15. Acceptance Plan
16. Contract Management Plan
17. Work Assignments
18. Status Reports
19. Minutes of Meetings
20. Change Requests
21. Escalations & Issue Mgt.
22. Sign-offs/ Completion Reports
23. Business Benefits Validation
24. Supporting Documentation (Solution, Technology, Specs etc.)

© Dhanu Kothari & Romeo Mitchell 2007

70

☐ *Dependency Chart*

The chart forms the basis for controlling project schedule and time. It is a result of defining activities, sequencing and estimating, and the resolution of mandatory, discretionary and external dependencies. It is the vehicle to identify critical vs. non-critical activities and assess scheduling options during the course of the project.

☐ *Baseline Schedule*

An optimum schedule is developed, based on firm resource commitments, resource skills, and constraints due to imposed dates, key events, external suppliers and assumptions. It is the result of an iterative process and constitutes the Baseline Schedule.

☐ *Deliverables/ Responsibility Matrix*

Also known as the RACI chart, it outlines for each activity the individual responsible for the end product, expected deliverables, the individual responsible for accepting the deliverable, completion criteria and target completion date.

☐ *Resource Plan*

The resources, skill levels and timing necessary for completing project deliverables forms the Resource Plan. It gets commitment from Resource Managers and is needed to determine gaps in skill levels and plan for training.

☐ *Financial Plan*

Cost estimating, cost budgeting and cost control requires a Financial Plan. It takes into consideration resource requirements, and provides cost estimates by milestone, cost baseline, spending plan and a cost management plan.

☐ *Risk Management Plan*

Risk factors that are likely to affect the project are identified. This is followed by impact assessment, risk mitigation strategies and contingency planning.

☐ *Project Quality Plan*

It addresses quality attributes and measurable criteria for the project deliverables as well as the Project Management process itself. It includes operational definitions, proposed tools and techniques, expected outputs, and a list of Quality Assurance and Quality Control measures to be adopted for the project.

☐ *Communication & Control Plan*

There should be a common understanding of the process to be used for reviewing and controlling the project. This plan formalizes the format and frequency of status reports, project reviews, follow-up procedures, and steps for escalating and resolving issues in a timely manner.

☐ *Change Management Plan*

It is the basis for managing Change Requests. Changes to the scope of the project could be caused due to external events, errors/omissions in specifications or need to include new value-adding features. It gives a framework for evaluating their impact on the scope, time, cost and quality of the project.

☐ *Acceptance Plan*

This outlines the various acceptance criteria associated with each deliverable, and the process to be followed for testing, review and sign-offs for the acceptance. Scope verification is an integral part of the Acceptance Plan and it formalizes acceptance of the project scope by the stakeholders.

☐ *Contract Management Plan*

It identifies the entire process for administering the contracts. It includes details regarding the scope of work, contractor evaluation and selection criteria, terms of the contract, administration process, acceptance criteria and approvals.

The outcome of the "Adapt" process is a Baseline Plan, a Baseline Schedule and a Recovery Roadmap which is an easy to follow visual presentation of the Recovery Plan. The Recovery Manager is now ready to assign the work to team members which is the subject of the next chapter "Assign Responsibilities and Delegate".

08   a4 – assign responsibilities & delegate

Project Recovery - The A^{10} Model©

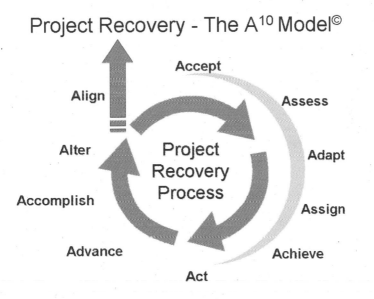

Once the revised Baseline Plan and Baseline Schedule are in place, the next process is the assignment and delegation of responsibilities. The main objectives of the "Assign" process are to clearly define responsibilities and get commitments that are essential for implementing the project plan and processes to achieve project goals. Acceptance of responsibility and personal commitment by team members are critical to building confidence and morale.

The Recovery Manager's focus must be oriented towards the future, with no commitment to the past. The task at hand is to "stop the bleeding" immediately and prevent further loss or damage as part of the overall recovery plan.

During this time, it is quite normal that there is a feeling of apprehension and uncertainty among team members about their future roles and responsibilities in the project. People tend to become defensive, they are insecure, there is skepticism and emotions run high. Therefore, the Recovery Manager must act quickly and fairly, and delegate work successfully.

The authority of the Recovery Manager is clear and explicit - to get the project under control and manage the recovery in accordance with the Recovery Plan. As such, the Recovery Manager is solely responsible for its success. The concept of joint responsibilities or co-Project Managers is not recommended in these situations. To exercise this authority, the Recovery Manager must have a clear understanding of all the players, as well as their roles and relationships with respect to the project.

One cannot expect to manage a successful recovery without understanding "Who is Doing What to Whom" in the project. The tool used for this is the post-assessment Project Organization Chart (Figure 8-A)

Organizing for Recovery

There are many key roles and functions associated with a project recovery. Typically, the basic roles include Recovery Steering Committee, Project Sponsor, Project Recovery Manager and the Project Manager.

Depending on the type and complexity of recovery, there are other roles such as Lead Designer, Client Manager, internal and external Stakeholders, Technical personnel, Developers, Quality Assurance experts, End Users, Support and maintenance personnel, Service Desk consultants and sub-Contractors. Each one of these roles is inherent to a recovery project and is performed by specific individuals who are responsible for the roles.

The very existence of many roles and responsibilities in a project gives rise to multiple objectives, conflicting opinions and competing priorities among the various parties. Add to that the challenges of dealing with different personalities, management styles, communication protocols, cultural differences and individual expectations, and you have the scenario for politics in Project Management.

Managing the politics of such an environment requires that the Recovery Manager act as a facilitator, mediator and a negotiator to ensure that the interaction among all of the players is effective and productive. Successful Recovery Managers leverage project politics effectively by ensuring that these roles are identified, defined and assigned to the project.

Of all the roles noted above, there are certain key roles that are absolutely vital in a successful recovery, and they are associated with Project Sponsor, Recovery Manager, Project Manager, Client Manager and Stakeholders. Without the active support, participation, commitment and "buy-in" of these critical roles, a successful recovery is not possible.

Figure 8-A

Organizing for Project Recovery

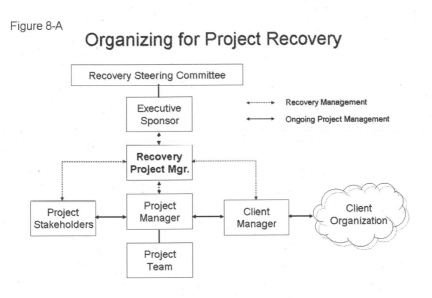

© Dhanu Kothari & Romeo Mitchell 2007

Defining Roles and Responsibilities

1. Recovery Steering Committee

Most organizations have a Management or Steering Committee that is made up of senior executives. The committee is responsible for establishing strategic direction and business goals. It defines and communicates management expectations and success indicators for strategic undertakings. It also provides timely resolution of strategic issues and conflicts.

In the case of recovery, a Recovery Steering Committee (RSC) is formed with core participants consisting of the Project Sponsor, Recovery manager, Project Manager and major stakeholders.

The RSC creates an enabling environment for accomplishing the recovery. It does this by setting policy guidelines for recovery decisions, directing participating functions and departments to follow the guidelines, assigning priorities and allocating needed resources, and finally, getting a consistent message regarding expectations, focus and objectives of the recovery.

The RSC is critical to the success of recovery in large organizations, especially if the scope or impact of the recovery cuts across functional boundaries within and outside the organization.

2. Project Sponsor

The role of the Project Sponsor is to represent the decisions of the Management or Steering Committee to the project. The Sponsor has a vision of the project and a vested interest in its success. While bringing passion to the project, the Sponsor ensures the availability of funds for the project, and continually monitors the project to see that it is aligned with the strategic objectives of the function, business and the organization.

The Sponsor insulates the Project Manager from high level politics in the organization, and serves as the focal point of escalation and resolution for issues outside the Project Manager's control. The Sponsor has the necessary clout and influence in the organization to drive the project across functional boundaries.

Finally, the Project Sponsor is an integral part of the Project Organization, not just a "figure head".

3. Recovery Manager

The Recovery Manager is an experienced Project Manager who is brought in on an interim basis to bring the derailed project back on track as soon as possible. With full authorization and support of the Sponsor, he/she drafts a Recovery Charter, prepares a new baseline plan for the project in accordance with the scope of the recovery, and obtains approval to implement it.

The Recovery Manager takes charge of the Project, and functioning as a Project Manager, implements the project structure, processes and tools that are required to reestablish the confidence of the client and key stakeholders, and bring stability to the project. During this time, the Recovery Manager also coaches the Project Manager and, when the project is stable, transfers responsibility back to the Project Manager for ongoing project management.

The Recovery Manager's role is similar to that of a medical specialist who performs diagnosis and provides necessary treatment to bring things under control, after which the responsibility for ongoing care and maintenance reverts to the general physician.

4. Project Manager

The Project Manager role represents the single point of responsibility for the success or failure of the project. He/She works with all stakeholders to define project goals, objectives, critical success factors and acceptance criteria. He manages the project scope, cost, and schedule while maintaining focus on project goals and objectives.

He identifies resource requirements, negotiates for priorities and resources, builds the project team and keeps it motivated towards achieving the goal. Above all, he sets expectations with the client regarding project goals and mutual responsibilities with respect to the project.

The Project Manager manages relationships and client expectations, institutes formal communication vehicles for project planning, updates and reporting, and is always one step ahead of potential problems and project risks.

He works with the client towards effective management of change through training and ongoing selling of the project. He escalates issues that are outside his control and seeks resolution. He is loyal to his organization, the client, the product, the profession and the people in his team.

Finally, the Project Manager provides leadership, a sense of purpose and motivation for the project team. In the case of recovery projects, the Project Manager gets coaching from the Recovery Manager while the project gets stabilized, and resumes responsibility for it when it is formally turned over.

5. Lead Designer/ Design Engineer/ Solution Architect

The Lead Designer role addresses the architecture, technology and design of the proposed solution. The role may be performed by a single individual or several individuals depending on the type or complexity of the project.

In a recovery situation, the subject of design is often a source of major challenge and conflict which can be attributed to defensive attitudes, individual pride associated with design approaches, personal egos or just a lack of documentation in many cases.

The Recovery Manager works with the Lead Designer to get an objective assessment of alternatives and technical risks for recovery, and proposes a recommended solution. The Lead Designer continually validates that the recovery solution will work as planned, and guides the development team towards meeting functional, performance and quality specifications based on the technology.

6. Other Stakeholders

A Stakeholder is simply anyone who has a "stake" in the outcome of the project. The term includes individuals, departments, functions or organizations that have a vested interest in the outcome of the project, and quite often, are impacted by it.

The stakeholder can be internal or external to the delivery and client's organizations. A stakeholder need not be actively involved in the project, nor have an explicit decision-making role in its conduct or progress - however, he may wield significant influence on the direction and in some cases, disruption of the project!

The Recovery Manager establishes a rapport with key stakeholders and gets them to acknowledge the need for recovery, and support the plan for recovery.

7. Client or Customer Manager

The Client Manager acts as the Project Manager's counterpart on the client side. He/She represents the client organization for decisions regarding all aspects that impact the client organization. These might include signoffs on requirements and ongoing deliverables, liaising with functional managers, coordinating internal activities, getting the buy-in at various stages of the project, managing change within the client environment and ensuring readiness for implementation.

The absence of an identified specific individual as a Client Manager is one of the major sources of project failures. The Client Manager is the individual who makes decisions and compromises, and negotiates on behalf of the client.

Simply stated, the Project Manager and the Client Manager need each other and are dependent on each other. They work hard to develop and sustain a trusting relationship. They are "joined at the hip" and work together towards a common goal.

Delegating Responsibility

A clear understanding of the key roles, relationships and responsibilities sets the stage for effective delegation, genuine acceptance and enthusiastic commitment. It is founded on the simple management principle that authority is exercised, responsibilities are delegated and commitments are accepted.

The person accepting commitments must clearly understand what the deliverables are, and who will be accepting them. For delegation to be effective, there must be a positive acknowledgement of commitment by the acceptor.

Deliverables provide the linkage between the delegation of responsibility and the acceptance of commitment. The vehicle to achieve effective delegation and communication is the RACI chart that is commonly used by the Recovery Manager.

The RACI Chart

Delegating work to team members and getting their enthusiastic commitment is a key function of Project Management. One of the tools for achieving effective delegation and related communication is a chart which derives its name RACI from four basic roles associated with it: Responsibility, Approval, Consultation and Information.

Figure 8-B

Project Recovery – RACI/RAM Chart

Work Package/ Deliverable	Recovery Roles and Responsibilities							
Project Roles	PM	RM	ES	ST1	ST2	Client	Team	Date
Conduct Initial Quick Scan	C	R	C					
Prepare Recovery Charter	C	R	A	I	I	I		
Do Compliance Quick Scans	C	R	A					
Conduct Proj. Health Check	C	R	A	I	I	I	C	
Prepare Assessment Plan	I	R	A					
Conduct Deep Dives	I	R					C	
Prepare Det. Assessment	I	R						
Develop Proj. Recovery Plan	C	R	A	I	I	I		
Execute the Recovery Plan	R	R	A	I	I	I		
Deliver Quick Wins	R	R	I	I	I	A		
Prepare new Proj. Baseline	R	C				A		
Enhance Proj Mgt. Pocesses	A	R	A	I	I	C	I	
Coach the Project Mgr.	A	R	I					
Review Project Stability & Transfer Responsibility to PM	A	R	C	I	I	C		
Manage Project as per the new Baseline	R		C	I	I	A		

PM-Project Mgr.   RM-Recovery Mgr.   ES-Exec. Sponsor   ST-Stakeholder
R : Responsible for the Deliverable   A : Accepts/ Approves the deliverable
C : Must be Consulted   I : Needs to be Informed

© Dhanu Kothari & Romeo Mitchell 2007

The RACI chart, also known as a Responsibility Assignment Matrix (RAM) is a powerful tool for clearly defining and delegating responsibilities. As illustrated in Figure 8-B, it is simply a matrix that consists of a list of deliverables, and a list of individuals along with their roles on the project. For each deliverable, you fill in the matrix by identifying:

- The individual responsible for creating the deliverable or ensuring that it is created and delivered (R)

- The individual who is accountable for approving or accepting the completed deliverable (A)

- The individual(s) who must be consulted, based on their knowledge and expertise relative to the deliverable(C)

- The individuals who need to be kept informed of any significant steps or events along the way (I).

Guidelines for using the RACI chart

1. Have a list of work packages and deliverables ready for discussion (These follow from the Work Breakdown Structure for the project).

2. Identify responsibility with a related business process. This provides the link between a purely technical perspective and its associated business context.

3. Get the team involved and decide upon the individuals and responsibilities to be assigned to the R,A,C and I roles.

4. Fill in the chart, working with each work package or deliverable at a time.

5. Include additional information regarding Target Date and Budget for each item.

6. Provide an initial draft for review by the participants, conduct 1-2 iterations to produce the final version.

Micro-management for Recovery

Contrary to the conventional Project Management principles, micro-management is essential during early stages of recovery. This is when the "inch stone" plan - that is the plan for the initial 2-4 weeks - is meticulously executed and monitored to ensure that delivery targets are met on a daily basis, and progress is demonstrated quickly.

Once the team has regained its confidence and credibility, then the Recovery Manager can slowly ease up on micro-management, and revert to the normal practice of managing by milestones and achieving goals by setting realistic targets.

The final RACI chart reflects the consensus of the team. It eliminates ambiguities with respect to responsibilities. It helps to develop cooperation among the team players who must work together to deliver a product. It minimizes the need for redundant communication and it makes everyone's role and commitments visible. It secures the team's participation in the decision-making process which ultimately builds individual commitment.

09   a5 - achieve goals by setting realistic targets

Project Recovery - The A^{10} Model©

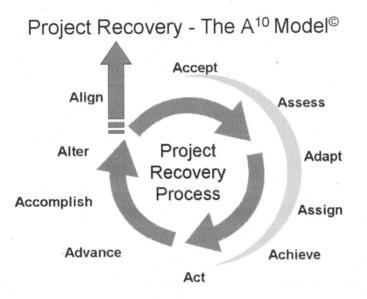

Align · Accept · Assess · Alter · Adapt · Accomplish · Assign · Advance · Achieve · Act

Project Recovery Process

The Recovery Manager follows certain guidelines and rules to manage the recovery. They include: a clear vision of recovery objectives, a decision-making process for sound decisions, a trusting environment, and skilled and motivated team members. Execution of the recovery plan begins with resolving the most important issues first, and "stop the bleeding".

There is an expectation to demonstrate quick and visible results, knowing that one does not have the luxury of time to implement an ideal solution. The recovery targets, therefore, have to be achievable, aggressive and realistic. They should be designed to ensure that steady and frequent milestones are achieved throughout the project, and especially in the early stages of the recovery. A recovery roadmap provides the means to attain the targets.

Executing the Recovery Plan

The major considerations in executing the Recovery Plan are:

- Adopting the vision for the "To Be" state of recovery
- Identifying the gap between "As Is" and "To Be" states
- Minimizing discussion of past events and history
- Focusing on business needs, recovery objectives and strategic alignment
- Conducting a review of needs vs. requirements
- Identifying the root causes at micro levels
- Evaluating alternatives and new solutions for recovery
- Preparing a cost justification
- Reviewing the project organization and redesigning it, if necessary
- Facilitating management of change

Developing an Implementation Roadmap

Once the decision has been made to implement a recovery, the Project Manager is expected to act expeditiously. There is not enough time to assess if all the requirements have been defined or whether the necessary resources will be available at the right time; rather, the challenge is to get the project done by the due date while battling the unknowns and constraints.

This is where the Implementation Roadmap comes in. It is similar to a model that an architect builds to help his clients visualize the final structure. The roadmap is a model that shows the flow of activities and events in a project from start to finish. It is a visual representation of activities, constraints and dependencies that show how we plan to get there, from here. Without the Roadmap, we wouldn't know where we are going and we certainly will never get there.

Every project must have a roadmap that articulates the flow of planned work from start to finish including major milestones, activities and the critical path. Preparation of the roadmap is a team effort requiring an exchange of ideas with healthy discussion among the team members. The roadmap is an excellent vehicle to gain the client's confidence and stakeholders' understanding of the issues and complexity of the project.

The roadmap also helps us to differentiate between planning and scheduling, and presents us with a bird's eye-view of the implementation process. The Recovery Manager knows how to leverage the roadmap as yet another tool to clearly differentiate between the "What" and "How" of recovery:

- *What we do* ... is driven by the project objectives and scope.

- *How it's done* ... is based on the standards, conventions, technology and industry practices for the project and your business.

- *What we commit to* ... is a result of negotiations based on availability of resources, risk tolerance and achievable and realistic deadlines. This is reflected in the project baseline schedule.

At the core of the roadmap for recovery, is the concept of managing with milestones.

Managing with Milestones

Milestones are like a series of markers or sign posts guiding you on the highway of your journey towards project completion. They tell you how far you've come, where you are on your journey and what the next marker is. They provide you with the assurance that you are headed in the right direction, and serve as intermediate goals that you can strive to accomplish.

Milestones give you and your team a continual sense of accomplishment as you progress from one goal to another. Simply stated, milestones are a series of intermediate targets, deliverables and goals that you accomplish one after another until the entire project is complete.

The use of milestones forces a sense of discipline on the project team, and when practiced with rigour and regularity, promotes a healthy work habit. Milestones serve as checkpoints along the project's journey, validate key deliverables and accomplishments, and provide a virtual picture of progress towards the goal. The dreaded last minute "surprises" are limited and addressed as they occur for each milestone, instead of waiting until it is too late.

Successful projects are managed by milestones. They serve as significant events in the progression of the project. They provide meaning and purpose to the daily work we do in context of the overall project.

Above all, milestones serve as an affirmation of the project's progress as planned and continually boost the confidence and morale of the team. An example of a dependency diagram with an implementation roadmap for a complex recovery is shown in Figure 9.

Figure 9

Project Recovery Roadmap

© Dhanu Kothari & Romeo Mitchell 2007

Executing the Inch-Stone Plan

An Inch-Stone plan is a subset of the overall baseline plan for recovery, and it is developed on a rolling basis that covers a 5-10 days period as the project progresses. A milestone is further broken down into miniature milestones that are associated with very small but measurable accomplishments.

The concept of an inch-stone plan is similar to executing short term turn-around projects such as maintenance of plant equipment, office relocations, server migrations etc. where a "time-critical" project is broken down into the smallest of details, meticulously planned and rigorously executed. It is essentially a micro-plan with a micro-schedule. Inch-stone planning forces the team's attention on making progress in small incremental steps as part of the overall plan.

There are many advantages to the inch-stone approach. It helps to prevent a recurrence of major problems during the recovery. It provides objective evidence of progress and improvement in control. It serves as input for establishing realistic and achievable targets for further activities.

Finally, with respect to the client, it shifts the focus of discussion to where it needs to be - on what has been accomplished as opposed to what was not delivered.

To summarize, the key points in achieving recovery are to:

- Generate confidence by delivering quick results
- Focus on the critical path
- Establish milestones 1-2 weeks apart with clear deliverables
- Get the client's signoff for each deliverable
- Micro-manage with an "Inch-stone" plan to gain confidence
- Stay away from a "Big Bang" implementation
- Continually measure & validate business benefits along the way

Recovery - a TEAM Effort

The dependency chart makes it easy to visualize the steps in executing the project. It serves as a tool for educating the client and management in terms of understanding what is involved in the project; how it needs to be done; what is most critical; what is driving the completion date; what the alternatives and associated risks are; and where to put the resources. It provides a bird's eye view of the project and serves as a tool for further negotiations and justification for resources.

Executing the inch-stone plan is a team effort. The Recovery Manager gets the team involved during planning, discusses ideas and gets the client's and team members' input to arrange and rearrange the sequence of activities until a broad consensus has been reached. The process makes everyone aware of the critical path and helps everyone to understand the background and rationale for the decisions. When you get them involved, you are one step closer to getting their commitment.

Simply stated, the inch-stone plan translates the vision into a process. It shows the way for filling the gap between promises and results. The successful execution of the recovery roadmap depends on an effective decision-making process, which the subject of the next chapter: "Act Consistently and Decisively".

10   a6 – act consistently and decisively

Project Recovery - The A^{10} Model$^©$

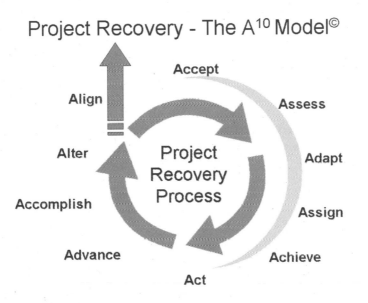

A sound and consistent decision making process is vital for a successful recovery. Such a process is open to deploying a variety of problem solving techniques, and it focuses on key problems to be resolved. It enables the Recovery Manager to act decisively on set goals and moves the project forward. It should be noted that the process is expected to be iterative and could result in a review and adjustment of recovery targets established in the "inch-stone" plan.

The Project Manager is constantly faced with making decisions related to changes, escalations, priorities, resources, risks and technologies. How does one arrive at a decision that is practical, sound and viable? The Project Manager achieves this by following a team process for analysis and synthesis of available data, getting the team to participate in discussing alternatives and their impact, and finally, by taking a decision.

Decision Making and Decision Taking

A good decision making process is ideally based on reasoning skills, team participation and arriving at a consensus. The process, however, must be followed by taking a decision and acting upon it. There is a fundamental difference between decision making and decision taking. Decision making is a process that encourages team involvement, participation and exchange of different viewpoints that ultimately lead to better decision making.

On the other hand, decision taking is a singular act by an individual based on facts, assessment and intuition, and accepting responsibility for its consequences. The Project Manager follows and guides a decision making process, and takes responsibility for whatever decision is taken. Figure 10-A illustrates the 3 stages in a decision making model.

Figure 10-A

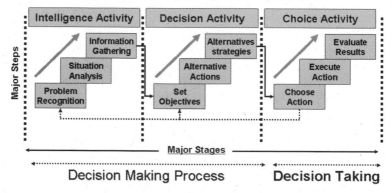

Project Recovery & Decision-Making

Decision-making is a process ... involves stakeholders.
Decision-taking is a formal act by an individual
who takes responsibility for the decision.

© Dhanu Kothari & Romeo Mitchell 2007

Guidelines for Decision-Making

There are certain guidelines that lead to sound decisions. It is often said that "Half of all decisions fail" because they ignore the real problem, try to solve the wrong problem or are developed without the involvement and participation of key stakeholders. This is especially critical in project recovery as its success depends on the enthusiastic acceptance and implementation of recovery decisions. The guidelines are:

1. Focus on the desired outcome of the recovery and then work backwards to define the problems to be resolved in the context of project objectives and scope. The purpose of recovery is to achieve the desired outcome, not simply to address a problem.

2. Encourage a creative thought process by involving the project team and stakeholders in the decision making process. This will lead to better decision making based on understanding different ideas, options and perspectives. Research shows that group decisions are better than individual decisions.

3. Include the stakeholders who are impacted by, or have a vested interest in the project outcome. Their involvement in the decision making process will lead to their "buy-in" of the decision and the commitment to implementing it. Consultation leads to commitment.

4. Identify the rationale, results and risks associated with a decision. The rationale deals with the "why", results focus on the "how" and risks help you prepare for the "what if". Decision making involves working with ambiguities, assumptions, risks and consequences.

5. Make a final choice and take the decision. Begin the implementation of your decision immediately, resulting in an immediate demonstration that progress is being achieved through small, concrete and meaningful steps towards the recovery.

Decision Making Tool Set

The Recovery Manager has a variety of tools and techniques that can be adapted to address complicated, difficult situations, and uses the ones most appropriate for the situation. Effective decision making consists of three components that deal with understanding the problem, analyzing alternatives and making a choice as shown in Figure 10-B. They are:

- Intelligence Activity - consisting of problem recognition, situational analysis and information gathering

- Decision Activity - consisting of setting objectives, and evaluating alternative actions and strategies

- Choice Activity - consisting of choosing a course of action, executing it and evaluating the outcome

Figure 10-B

Tools for Decision Making

Intelligence Tools

Appreciation – 5 Ws
Cash Flow Analysis
Cause & Effect
Drill Down
PEST Analysis
Porter's Five Forces
Risk Analysis
SWOT Analysis
Systems Relationships
Value Analysis

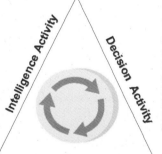

Intelligence Activity

Decision Activity

Decision Tools

Cost Benefit Analysis
Decision Trees
Force Field Analysis
Grid Analysis
Paired Comparison
Pareto Analysis
PMI
Six Thinking Hats

Choice Activity
Choice Tools
Risk Assessment & Risk Tolerance
Consequence assessment and risk Planning
Execution Planning

© Dhanu Kothari & Romeo Mitchell 2007

Tools for Intelligence Activity

These sets of tools are designed to collect, formulate and present data related to complex and difficult situations, and they provide the basis for further analysis and discussion. The Recovery Manager knows how and when to use the tools most effectively:

- *5 Whys* - The 5 why's technique typically refers to the practice of asking, five times, why the failure has occurred in order to get to the root cause of the problem. These series of questions provide a framework for further understanding by drilling down into specific details. They also provide a relationship between different root causes of a problem, and are most beneficial when problems involve human factors and interactions.

- *Cash Flow Analysis* - This tool is used for predicting the viability of a financial decision for a project or business. It consists of a model that takes into account the movement of cash such as inflow and outflow, and it helps to analyze the profitability of a project under varying sets of circumstances.

- *Cause and Effect diagram* - Also known as the Fish-bone or Ishikawa diagram, it is a structured process for conducting thorough analysis, categorizing potential causes in an orderly way and identifying the root causes of a problem. The categories often consist of 4Ms (Methods, Machines, Materials, Manpower), 4Ps (Place, Procedure, People, Policies), and 4Ss (Skills, Systems, Supplier, Surroundings) or any combination thereof.

- *Drill Down* - It consists of breaking complex problems into smaller, manageable parts and leads to deeper understanding of issues and factors that contribute to it. Any lack of information becomes visible and provides focus for further research. This exercise is similar to developing a Work Breakdown Structure where a project is broken down into a number of components.

- *PEST Analysis* - PEST stands for the big picture surrounding Political, Economic, Socio-cultural and Technological environment. The analysis starts with a brainstorming exercise to identify major trends that are associated with each category. An understanding of the trends and associated influences can help towards planning an optimum level of recovery.

- *Porter's Five Forces* - It is designed for analyzing competitive power or advantage based on five criteria, namely, Supplier

Power, Buyer Power, Threat of Substitution, Threat of New Entry and Competitive Rivalry. It provides a way of analyzing the balance of power related to the major considerations that impact the issue being considered.

- *Risk Analysis* - It consists of identifying, evaluating and quantifying potential risks related to Technical, Implementation, Management, Organization or other issues that might significantly impact the outcome of the project, and planning a risk management strategy.

- *SWOT Analysis* - It is used for understanding a project's or organization's strengths, weaknesses, opportunities and threats. The outcome from a SWOT Analysis enables organizations to focus on strengths, minimize weaknesses, address threats, and take the greatest possible advantage of opportunities available.

- *System Interrelationships* - Provides a way of understanding the workings of complex and inter-dependent relationships, and shows how changes in one might affect another part of the system. In a typical recovery project, such analysis will possibly include a discussion of the management of change associated with the recovery.

- *Value Chain Analysis* - This approach looks at work that is delivered or performed from the customer's viewpoint and focuses on maximizing the value from the customer's perspective. For example, in a recovery environment, the customer value will likely consist of speed to bring the project under control, client confidence, commitment to recovery plan and evidence of timely delivery etc. The Value Chain consists of three steps: Activity analysis, Value Analysis and Evaluation & Planning.

Tools for Decision Activity

These sets of tools are used to identify possible alternatives, evaluating the pros and cons of each including possible risks and consequences, and choosing a course of action that is best suited for the project.

- *Cost Benefit Analysis* - This is a widely used technique for deciding whether to undertake a project or implement a change. It compares value of the anticipated benefits with associated costs, and provides an insight into the financial viability of a project. It is a major consideration for deciding the strategy for dealing with a troubled project and the scope of project recovery.

- *Decision Trees* - These provide an effective method for decision making by laying out the problem, possible courses of action, value associated with each outcome and the probabilities of achieving them. They provide a balanced picture of risks and rewards associated with each option and likely outcomes.

- *Force Field Analysis* - It helps in understanding the organizational dynamics and forces supporting or opposing a situation or a plan. Based on the analysis, the Project Manager can put together a strategy to strengthen and leverage the supporting forces, and persuade or sell the opposing forces. Project Managers often use this tool to conduct Stakeholder Analysis and gain their support.

- *Grid Analysis* - This is most effective where you have a number of good alternatives and many factors to take into account. Each one of the factors is associated with a relative importance or weight. The analysis provides a final score for each option which serves as further input to decision making.

- *Paired Comparison Analysis* - This is used for comparing several courses of actions against one another, and selecting an optimum solution. It is particularly useful when objective data is not available or there are conflicting demands and limited resources.

- *Pareto Analysis* - Often referred to as the "80/20" principle, it provides the means to identify all the problems associated with a situation, and shows the most important problem to solve. It is a formal technique for identifying issues and implementing changes that will give the biggest benefits. The technique is useful where many possible causes are contributing to a situation, and courses of action are available to address the situation.

- Plus/Minus/Implications (PMI) - It provides a means for weighing the pros, cons and implications of a decision. It is often used to validate a course of action and check if it worth taking in light of the weighted results and benefits or risks associated, with possible implications.

- *Six Thinking Hats* - Developed by Edward de Bono, this tool helps to look at a decision or a situation from many perspectives such as factual data, emotional responses, negative considerations, optimistic viewpoints, creative approaches and the processes adopted for discussion and exchange of ideas. It promotes the use of a variety of approaches in dealing with the project's clients and stakeholders.

Tools for Choice Activity

These tools assist the Recovery Manager to make an assessment of potential risks that are associated with a decision and their impact on business. The final decision is made based on the level of risk that is acceptable for the project and the business. There are risks associated with every decision. They need to be identified, evaluated and quantified in terms of their impact on the business in the event of their occurrence. A decision is made based on the assessment of consequences, and a plan is developed to execute the decision.

To summarize, decision making processes that are based on participation and involvement of stakeholders generally lead to sound decisions. They also lead to stakeholders' acceptance, buy-in and commitment to implement the decisions. The key to obtaining commitment is to have people involved, included and have their input acknowledged and considered.

The ultimate responsibility for choosing a course of action and taking the decision rests with the Recovery Manager, who must also ensure that it is communicated and followed through effectively for successful implementation.

11 a7- advance the recovery through communication

Project Recovery - The A^{10} Model©

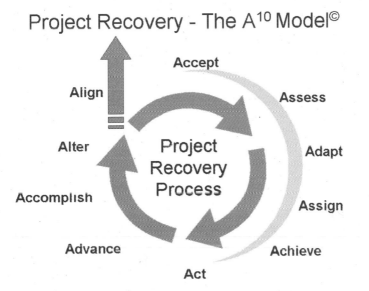

The Recovery Manager is faced with many challenges and forces that prevent the successful completion of a project. The client is upset, the team is frustrated, the morale is low, there is wide spread skepticism and considerable negativity, often associated with finger-pointing in all directions.

Under these circumstances, effective communication is the only vehicle available to the Recovery Manager to manage stakeholders' expectations, and hold the team together while motivating everyone towards advancing the recovery effort.

There are, however, many organizational realities that can derail project communications.

Communication Challenges

1. *Messages get interpreted, re-interpreted or simply lost in translation.*

   This can happen due to the sheer number of players and multiple communication channels. Add to this the complexity arising from individual personality, attitude, agenda, game plan perceptions and motivation with respect to the project. Language, however clearly spoken or written, is still an imperfect medium for achieving 100% success in communication.

2. *Organization culture forces people to be optimistic.*

   Many organizations have an "institutionalized" project culture that demands only positive and optimistic feedback on their projects. Such a culture refuses to acknowledge the existence of risks and potential problems, and demands that the Project Manager puts a positive twist on them, regardless of the consequences. The end result is that problems are buried instead of being raised and resolved in the open.

3. *No one likes to be the bearer of bad news.*

   Some organizations have a culture of fear or intimidation that has filtered all the way down from the top. Such a culture thrives on, and expects a "yes" mentality from its team members, and contributes to a threatening environment. Team members in this culture keep their heads down for fear of punishment rather than voice the issues.

   No one wants to know the facts and real issues until, of course, the project turns into a disaster. There are many examples of projects, often cited as "the dead fish of failure" where the objectives, expectations and success criteria are utterly unattainable from the outset, but the work still goes on for lack of an honest conversation.

4. *Communication Overload leads to Chaos, Confusion and Consternation*

The ease of communicating with various tools can result in over communication. As team size increases, so do the potential channels of communication. In many projects, there is often a lack of protocol for communication. The end result is wasted time, duplication of effort, and detracting people from doing what they are supposed to do. For communication to be effective, it must be clear, concise and complete, and it must be specific and meaningful to the recipients.

5. *Politics, Politics, Politics ..... a fact of life.*

Project Communication is subject to, and suffers from the state of organizational politics, especially when it is the only game in town. In such organizations, teamwork and trust are on the back-burner until departmental or individual rivalries are settled. Organizations suffer from, and quite often, thrive on politics that include conflicting objectives, competing goals and confusing priorities resulting in many opinions, disagreements, lack of commitment, personal biases and employee dissatisfaction. That's the nature of organizations and it often gets worse when faced with troubled projects.

Consequently, it is the Recovery Manager's job to motivate all the players to move in the same direction with respect to the project. The Recovery Manager, therefore, knows how to practice politics in a positive sense, leverage it to influence events and people, and to steer the recovery towards its objectives and intended outcome. It consists of skills required to get someone's buy-in, negotiate for resources, manage change requests, handle team conflicts, champion the cause, seek budget approvals, and coach the Project Manager. The Recovery Manager must have a strong communication strategy and the organizational savvy to get ideas & recommendations accepted.

Communication Strategies

A well defined communications strategy is vital for a successful recovery. It encompasses all the project stakeholders that are impacted by the outcome of the project, or have a vested interest in the project. This includes project sponsors, project managers, team members, suppliers, contractors, consumers and business decision makers.

Since a project success or failure is ultimately judged by stakeholders, not project managers, it is important that the communication strategy is designed to manage these relationships as shown in Figure 11.

Figure 11

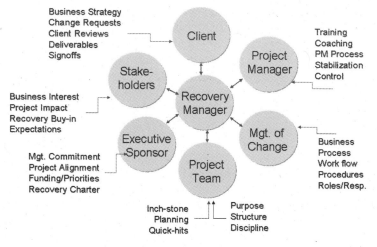

Project Recovery Interfaces & Communications

© Dhanu Kothari & Romeo Mitchell 2007

There are three steps to manage project stakeholders effectively:

1) Stakeholder Identification - Identifying the project stakeholders and how they will be affected by the project.

2) Stakeholder Prioritization - Ranking their importance based on the stakeholder's interest, influence and impact on the project's success.

3) Stakeholder Analysis - Understanding and mapping of stakeholders' motives and expectations for the project.

Based on these, the Recovery Manager develops a stakeholder communication strategy that includes the content and flow of information to meet their needs and objectives. The strategy, however, can only be successful if it has the support of senior management (e.g. project sponsor) and based on the honesty and integrity of the Recovery Manager which starts with "Fierce and Crucial Conversations":

Fierce and Crucial Conversations

A research study conducted by VitalSmarts, indicates that a vast majority of projects fail because people don't speak up. They are afraid to hold "crucial" conversations, the ones that need to occur when the stakes are high, emotions run strong, and opinions vary.

The study identified five types of conversations that are critical to a project's success, and why most project managers, team members and sponsors seem to do everything they can to avoid them. "One of the keys to successful project management is holding the right conversations on the right issues at the right times", concludes the study.

Projects rarely follow scripted performances according a plan; rather, they are a series of challenges, ongoing changes and continuing conflicts to be resolved with effective communications and "conversations".

Projects suffer when team members fail to have the crucial conversations they need to have. Recovery Managers should know how to confront the issues, bring them out into the open and develop a plan to address them. They do this by:

1. Challenging arbitrary deadlines, inadequate resources and unrealistic expectations that set up a project failure.

2. Confronting "Figurehead" sponsors that fail to provide leadership, political clout, time, or energy required to drive the project in the organization.

3. Questioning the manipulation of project priorities that often result in ambiguous agreements, scope creep and resource constraints.

4. Insisting on open discussion in the team so that bad news or problems are not swept under the rug, but tabled for discussion without fear of consequences or reprisals.

5. Dealing with non-committed team members who are unwilling or incapable of supporting the project.

In fact, these are the very factors that get projects into trouble in the first place. One cannot expect to recover from a troubled project by continuing with the same pattern of behaviour. The Recovery Manager is expected to address, influence and change them for the better, in order to achieve a successful recovery. Visual tools provide a powerful yet easy to use solution to effect the change.

Visual Tools for a Visible Recovery

A picture is worth a thousand words! People communicate through words, but they think and feel in images. A vast amount, estimated at 80%, of Recovery Manager's time and effort is expended towards communicating - activities such as selling, presenting, persuading, motivating, reviewing, meeting, negotiating, conferencing, reporting and updating on the project. The impact of these activities and overall communication becomes much enhanced and effective with the use of visual control tools.

Control tools are visual indicators that tell us at a glance how various aspects of the recovery effort are planned to be done, and whether they are deviating from the plan. The purpose is not just to report on status or history, but be able to determine immediately whether the project parameters are in standard conditions or deviating from them. They are designed to bring out issues and steer team efforts to address them.

Visual management tools have several benefits: They facilitate communication and sharing that enables fast and accurate decision making; they improve communication; they promote a common and consistent understanding about the process, flow and status of the project maintain alignment; they bring a sense of urgency to the collection of project data and dissemination of information; and they create a sense of team integration. And finally, they don't hide problems!

Visual charts and management tools, often located in a Project War Room setting, act as the nerve centre of recovery operations. Some examples of charts and tools for visual communication are: Work Breakdown Structure, Project Organization chart, Dependency chart, RACI chart, Milestones and Deliverables chart, Schedule and Cost chart, Rolling Risk Analysis, Solution Architecture diagrams, Change Orders statistics etc. These are powerful tools to achieve effective and successful communication in a project environment.

Finally, Recovery Managers know how to develop and implement an effective communication strategy. The strategy should be designed to engage the client and stakeholders throughout the project and keep them informed on accomplishment, issues, challenges, opportunities and deviations on the project. It should ensure timely and relevant communication directed upwards, sideways and downwards in the project organization, based on impact, interests and influences of the stakeholders. It must foster and nurture a culture of honest feedback and open sharing of information.

The purpose of communication is to bring out problems, not hide them. This is accomplished by using a variety of communication tools based on written, verbal, non-verbal, electronic and visual aids that are appropriate for the project environment. With the framework for successful communication in place, the Recovery Manager begins the task to "Accomplish Stability for Transitioning".

Recommended Tools

- Project Communication Matrix
- Project Communication Plan
- Project Recovery Roadmap
- Visual Charts (WBS, RACI, Project Organization)

12 a8 – accomplish stability for transitioning

Project Recovery - The A^{10} Model©

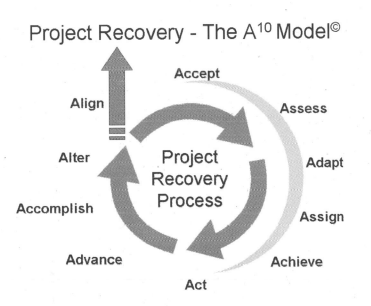

Recovery Management differs significantly from conventional project management. The objective of recovery is to help the Project Manager regain control of a troubled project and to re-establish a sense of order and stability in the project.

As such, it should be clearly understood that the role of the Recovery Manager is not to replace the Project Manager. Rather, it is to coach, guide and support the Project Manager in establishing a functioning, stable project environment, and having achieved this, to then fully pass on the reins to the Project Manager.

Indicators of Stability

Achieving stability is a pre-requisite for turning over project responsibility. How does one define stability in a project environment? There are several indicators:

☐ Project Management processes and procedures (the plan, the methods, the tools etc.) are in place, accepted by stakeholders, followed consistently and produce results. This includes everything from managing meetings, processing change orders, issuing status reports, resolving issues and documenting decisions. Some examples of a stable process are:

- A basic project management methodology
- A protocol and schedule for regular review meetings
- Use of standard project management tools and templates
- Agreed processes for decision making, escalation and resolution

☐ The client has received 3-4 intermediate and meaningful deliverables that demonstrate the effectiveness of recovery.

☐ There is a growing confidence among stakeholders and team members that the project is under control. The attitude of defensiveness and "blame game" has evolved into inter-dependence and trust among team members.

☐ The Project Manager and team members are confident that they can deliver as per the revised scope and schedule

☐ Post recovery roles are clearly defined and accepted by stakeholders and team members

Achieving Stability

The following guidelines are suggested for achieving stability:

1. Insist on following the discipline of Project Management. It may appear to be time consuming in the early stages, but it is worthwhile, in order to break away from the recovery syndrome.

2. Look after the team. They are all you've got to work with. Don't start off by "shooting" the project team or asking for greater effort and sacrifice from the project team. Rather, inspire them by reframing the project, redefining the scope and repairing stakeholder relationships.

3. Sell it to the team; they will rise to the occasion. Promote and facilitate team building and trust. Isolate or remove individuals with negative attitudes. Confidence and stability require an enthusiastic and positive response from team members. Clarify and redefine, if necessary, their roles and responsibilities.

4. Identify a set of immediate deliverables that are important and meaningful to the business. Set the stage for a common understanding of expectations, and begin to deliver. Make the client aware of what is working well, what was delivered and the business value of what they received.

5. Document decisions regarding scope, cost, risk and recommendations. Follow the precept "If it's not documented, it doesn't exist!" meticulously. Finally, do forward planning as it relates to Risk Management pertaining to Technical, Implementation, Management and Organizational aspects of the project.

Ensuring Stability - Forward Planning

Identifying genuine and relevant risks at any stage of the project requires a disciplined approach for discussion of ideas, analysis and synthesis of data. It is all the more critical in a recovery environment since a moderate risk event can easily disrupt the flow and outcome of recovery.

One way to manage critical risks is by analyzing and grouping them into four categories such as Technology, Implementation, Management and Organizational (TIMO) and identifying the top two or three risks for each category that could jeopardize the outcome of the project. This approach is illustrated in Figure 12 below.

1. *Technology Risks*

There are many sources of risks related to technology. These include the use of new or unproved technology, timely availability of technology, its integration with other solution components, supplier's capability to deliver the technology, and the time required to become familiar with it.

2. *Implementation Risks*

The primary sources of risk related to implementation are lack of skilled resources, scheduling conflicts, changes to project priorities, readiness for implementation, management of organizational and process change, and the transition to operations following project implementation.

3. *Management Risks*

Management risks can generally be attributed to ambiguous requirements, differences in expectations, lack of common understanding about project objectives and the absence of buy-in from functional managers and stakeholders. A major source of management risks is the lack of commitment and priority for the project by those who are most impacted by it.

4. *Organizational Risks*

The factors that contribute to organizational risks are: resistance to change, lack of enthusiasm and low morale among the team members, adversarial relationship between the Project Manager and the Client Manager, scepticism among union representatives, and a general absence of trust among the project players. Quite often, this is a reflection of the culture of the organization.

The Project Manager's failure to recognize, identify and manage these risks, in both the delivery and client organizations, can defeat the best laid plans for the project and result in severe consequences for the project.

Risk Mitigation & Contingency Planning

An assessment of risks requires a culture of openness where team members are encouraged to discuss them. A project environment where people feel threatened to discuss the risks and consequences generally ends up in failure. Recovery Managers are experienced in applying various strategies for mitigating risks: accept the risk, avoid the risk, reduce the risk or transfer the risk.

There are costs and consequences associated with each strategy resulting in what is known as the Expected Monetary Value (EMV) which is used as a guideline for decision making. The Project Manager's responsibility is to analyze the strategies and recommend the appropriate one to management for approval.

Figure 12

Risk Assessment for Recovery

New Technology. Timing & Availability
Integration Issues, Learning Curve
Technical Risks

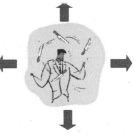

Organizational Risks
Scepticism
Low morale
Lack of Trust
Lack of enthusiasm
Resistance to change

Implementation Risks
Lack of skills
Project priorities
Speed of Recovery
Scheduling conflicts
Management of Change

Management Risks
Executive Sponsorship, Stakeholder buy-in
Recovery Expectations, Business Value

© Dhanu Kothari & Romeo Mitchell 2007

The ultimate decision to accept a specific risk and strategy rests with the management, while the responsibility to develop the plan and manage the risk rests with the Project Manager. The key is to ensure that one has an up to date risk management plan.

Managing Risks – A Simple Approach

1. Risk Description: Description of Risk – What is the risk?
2. Risk Source: Where & When is it likely to occur?
3. Risk Causes: What are the likely causes?
4. Risk Symptoms: What are the triggers?
5. Risk Impact: Critical, High, Medium or Low
6. Risk Amount: Effect on Project $ if no action is taken
7. Risk Probability: Probability of risk occurring if no action is taken
8. Risk Value: Estimated $ (Risk Amount X Probability)
9. Risk Response Strategy: Alternatives & Recommended Strategy (Avoid, Reduce, Transfer, or Accept)
10. Risk Response: Actions to implement Response Strategy
11. Response Cost: Estimated cost to execute the Response
12. Mgt. Approvals: Agreement on Strategy, Response & Cost

Regardless of the response strategy selected for the risk, the Project Manager is responsible for developing the response plan and managing it.

Leadership in Recovery Management

At the heart of project recovery, is a passion for Project Management. It has to do with clarity of purpose, change of direction, moving forward, improving project processes, inspiring the team and transforming the way we manage projects. It encompasses the skills and competencies of an outstanding Project Manager in the areas of business, management, technical and project management.

Recovery leadership is about willingness to take risks based on sound analysis and discussion, and making tough decisions. It knows how to change the direction of a troubled project by demonstrating quick short-term wins that are directly tied to business benefits. It achieves this by challenging and motivating the team while practicing the 5 Rs for effective team building – Respect, Recognition, Rewards, Rest and Recreation. It has the respect of stakeholders because of its integrity, and it knows how to leverage organizational politics to influence project outcome.

Above all, recovery is about showing a sense of urgency to bring things under control and raise the level of confidence among stakeholders and team members. The urgency is reflected in executing a plan that is built around the right project organization, stakeholders' interests and expectations, and team members' strengths. It begins with defining the direction for recovery, coaching the Project Manager, and ends with successful transitioning that alters the future direction of the project.

Recommended Tools

- ☐ Ongoing Project Risk Profile
- ☐ Risk Assessment
- ☐ Risk Management Plan
- ☐ Post Recovery Health Check

13　a9 – alter project direction through effective transition

Project Recovery - The A^{10} Model©

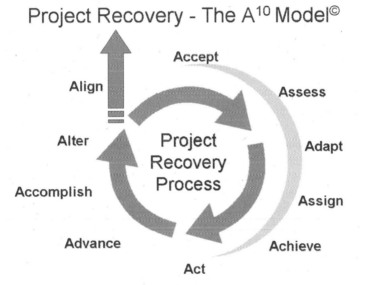

- Accept
- Assess
- Adapt
- Assign
- Achieve
- Act
- Advance
- Accomplish
- Alter
- Align

Project Recovery Process

Project Recovery is about significantly altering the direction of a project from a troubled state into a stable, functioning and predictable implementation. This is achieved through management of change, often called as Change Management, as it relates to people, processes and technology.

Managing change, however, is a challenging task. There are various organizational approaches to fixing the project, as well as dealing with related issues of scepticism and the low expectations often associated with people, and project-related resistance to the change, and the idea of change itself.

Management of change, as part of recovery, is achieved through three stages: Recovery Completion, Baselining for Ongoing Execution and Transition Management. The completion of recovery is validated by the indicators of stability described in the previous chapter.

The revised baseline takes into account the lessons of recovery, and redefines the project scope, objectives and deliverables so that they are achievable, and aligned with business needs. The Project Manager resumes responsibility for ongoing execution of the project in accordance with the revised baseline.

Transition Management, the process of introducing, internalizing and implementing required changes for the transition and beyond, continually takes place during recovery through the management of change and coaching.

Recovery Manager as a Change Agent

For the Recovery Manager, Change Management is the process of developing a planned approach to change the direction of the project. The approach ensures the enthusiastic participation of all stakeholders involved in the change and minimizes the risk of failure in implementing the change.

Although the change encompasses all aspects of the project, its success depends primarily on the human aspect of change with respect to culture, goals, objectives and teamwork in the project.

Recovery Managers, therefore, are also Change Agents who formulate the needed changes, market them internally, and implement them expeditiously for the project. Introducing changes for a troubled project deals with recognizing, confronting and dealing with typical issues of a dysfunctional team such as an overwhelming absence of purpose, structure, process, communication and cooperation.

A poorly managed change will invariably result in low morale, reduced productivity, increased anxiety, general confusion, defensiveness, and hostility. Change management begins with identifying specific stakeholders, understanding their expectations and concerns, getting their buy-in for a change of direction, engaging them in the project and creating a renewed vision for the project.

Management of Change

Successful change management consists of introducing it, internalizing it and finally, implementing it. Formulating the change and overcoming resistance to it is an integral part of introducing the change. Coaching is associated with internalizing, as it ensures that the planned change is accepted, understood and applied as intended.

Finally, integrating the change fully and anchoring it, as a final deliverable, into standard practices such as an organization's standard operating procedures (SOP) is the implementation. In a recovery environment, implementation of required changes occurs along with the transitioning of responsibility.

Three key steps are involved in managing a successful change for recovery:

☐ Initiate the Change
☐ Internalize the Change
☐ Implement the Change

Initiate the Change

Before a change is introduced, we need to understand the characteristics and nature of change in general, and the factors that contribute to its enthusiastic acceptance, outright rejection or passive observance.

- *Understanding Change*

Change is as much a matter of perception as it is of impact on those who are affected by it. If those affected by it perceive it as a threat to status quo, a disruption in established ways or a significant gap relative to their expectations of the project, then it is a major change. It is associated with people's beliefs that they have lost control over the project that might result in loss of face, power, prestige, self-worth or security. It is this negative perception that results in what is commonly known as "Resistance to Change".

It is important to recognize that resistance is an inherent characteristic of change, not to be confused with the people associated with it. It is a fact that a recovery means some kind of change in the project, that it is met with apprehension, that it is disruptive and uncomfortable, and that it won't happen until the project team is ready for it. Knowing how to deal with resistance to change is an essential skill for recovery management.

The key steps in understanding and clarifying the change are to:

☐ Determine the scope of need for change
☐ Frame the related issues in a larger context
☐ Validate support from senior management and
☐ key stakeholders
☐ Create a compelling message as to why change has to occur
☐ Formulate and communicate the vision behind the change

- *Resistance to Change*

Change fails because of failure to deal with resistance to change. The failure starts with unrealistic expectations, poor planning and estimating, inadequate communication, lack of stakeholder involvement and finally, lack of management accountability and support. Resistance to change manifests itself in a team member's self interest, misunderstanding, lack of trust, competing assignments, contradictory assessments and low tolerance levels to change.

How does the Recovery Manager overcome this challenge? The answer lies in one's skills and ability to influence people and exercise leverage in the organization - usually built upon a solid foundation of networking and relationships in the organization. It is said that the tendency to resist change is often based on emotions and a fear of the unknown.

People resist change not because they want to, but because they are uncertain as to how it will impact them. This is why managing the psychology of change is a key success factor in managing change. Some easy steps to accomplish this are to identify project champions, get the users positively engaged and involved, and to make the change personal by articulating its impact at the individual level.

- *Coping with Change*

A successful introduction of change must be accompanied with training and communication that is designed to assist people to cope with the change. It includes a compelling vision and a clear statement of objectives and rationale for doing it. It conveys a sense of urgency, and presents the costs, penalties and risks if there is no action taken. Communication, training and readiness are at the core of its success. Training prepares them for the change, and communication keeps them motivated for doing their part in it as active participants.

Internalize the Change

The second part of managing change is to ensure that it is fully internalized by those who are associated with it, and is institutionalized as part of ongoing processes. This can only happen with adequate support, on the job training/coaching and ongoing mentoring.

As such, the Recovery Manager's goal is not to replace the Project Manager, take charge of the project and finish it by himself. Rather, it is to coach the Project Manager while maintaining sufficient professional detachment so that there is no ambiguity about the ultimate responsibility for the success or failure of the project.

- *Coaching Principles*

Coaching involves working one-on-one with the Project Manager. It starts early in the assessment with the Project Manager's agreement that the project is worthy of recovery, and that such a recovery is possible.

At the heart of coaching is the need for an open and frank discussion based on mutual respect and trust. Without trust, there is no coaching. Coaching is both personal and situational as it relates to the Project Manager's interaction with management, clients, sponsors and team members.

Coaching is ongoing and time-sensitive. To be effective, it starts with planning and briefing to get ready for a situation, and ends with an analysis soon after the event in question has taken place. It requires discussion and debriefing around what worked particularly well and why, and what didn't and why.

Coaching identifies new skills, reinforces the right skills and continually validates expected improvements related to an individual's skills and behaviour. Finally, it underlines a commitment by the Recovery and Project Managers to impart, improve and internalize the positive coaching experience.

Figure 13 illustrates the key criteria for successful coaching. They are: Trust building, Shared commitment, Skills enhancement, Internalizing and consistent use of Lessons learned.

Figure 13
Management of Change
Initiate, Internalize, Implement

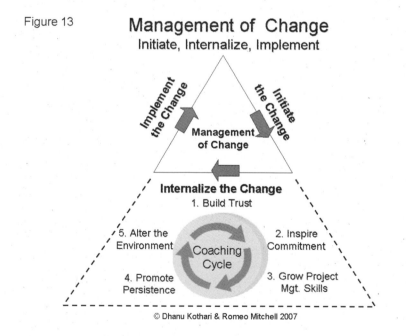

© Dhanu Kothari & Romeo Mitchell 2007

118

- *Coaching Dimensions*

Coaching is primarily focused on two areas: Skills and Behaviour. Skills can be acquired, refined or taught while behaviour is changed through acceptance, coaching and understanding. Skills focused coaching encompasses:

(1) Learning - where the Project Manager lacks the skills required to deal with a situation

(2) Doing - where the individual has the skills but doesn't know how to apply them and

(3) Debriefing - regarding an interaction or a situation to learn how it was handled, understand what worked well and capture the lessons learned.

Behaviour focused coaching deals with achieving change in behaviour, especially with respect to applying lessons learned during coaching. As an example, managing effective meetings is a skill that can be learned, while causing or promoting disruption in meetings is a trait of behaviour that needs to be changed based on debriefing.

3. Implement the Change

The third and final part of managing change is to implement it successfully. During this stage, the Recovery Manager must demonstrate bias towards action, maintain a high level of productivity, manage physical or emotional stress in the team, and demonstrate quick business benefits as a result of the change.

The Recovery Manager moves on as soon as the project is stabilized and the Project Manager feels confident about the project. This is formally accomplished through the following steps:

- Setting up a process for ongoing management of the project
- Developing a Transition Checklist in conjunction with the Project Manager

- Formalizing a turnover "Handshake" through a "Transition" meeting attended by the Project Manager, Project Sponsor and Key Stakeholders

Quite often, the changes implemented during recovery are worth incorporating into the overall project management practices of the organization to prevent recurrence of troubled projects. The Recovery Manager identifies rationale for supporting the change and the barriers to sustaining it, and influences the organization to permanently embrace the change by implementing a structure for Project Governance, Project Portfolio Management (PPM) and a Project Management Office (PMO).

Communication is crucial to the success of change management. It occurs throughout the planning and implementation of the changes. It is intended to clearly describe the benefits of how the changes will affect everyone. It fosters support and buy-in of the changes through involvement of team members, and enthusiastic support from project champions.

The Recovery Manager gets the clients and stakeholders engaged in the process, demonstrates quick business benefits from the change, and incorporates the lessons learned from managing the changes. Managing the psychology of change is as important as implementing the change itself.

Recommended Tools

- Project Assessment
- Stakeholder Analysis
- Change Management Plan
- Transition Plan
- Transition Checklist
- Formal Turnover and signoff

14 a10 – align for ongoing execution and targeted success

Project Recovery - The A^{10} Model$^©$

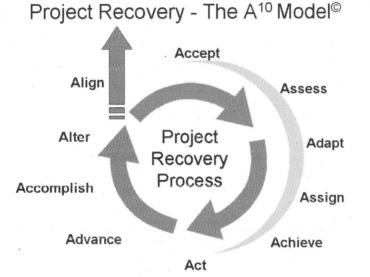

Accept

Align

Assess

Alter

Project Recovery Process

Adapt

Accomplish

Assign

Advance

Achieve

Act

There are several factors in a project that lead it into a troubled state. These include ongoing industry pressures due to accelerated implementations, restructuring and downsizing, mergers and acquisitions, faster technology obsolescence, and the use of new and unproven technologies.

Furthermore, the project environment itself continues to change rapidly as organizations struggle to embrace new "Projectized" cultures with a trend towards deploying distributed, outsourced and virtual teams. When combined with poor planning and a lack of Project Management discipline, these forces continue to ferment seeds of trouble in projects, and result in an increased demand for rampant recovery.

The lessons learned from project recovery should ideally result in addressing the root causes that contributed to the need for a recovery. Next, it involves setting up policies, processes and procedures that are aligned with organizational goals for the ongoing execution of projects.

The Recovery Manager, while dealing with a specific troubled project, also influences and steers the organization towards adopting a management approach that includes four key areas. These are:

- Strategic Planning
- Project Governance
- Project Portfolio Management (PPM)
- Enterprise Project Management Office (EPMO)

Strategic Planning

Strategic Planning articulates an organization's enterprise-wide vision which in turn filters down to lines of business (LOBs), clients and users resulting in operational plans. It consists of a framework for building a strategy that encompasses a 3-5 year vision.

The vision is then checked for reasonableness using the SWOT (Strengths, Weaknesses, Opportunities and Threats) analysis to see if it is realistic and achievable. It is then translated into a corporate plan which in turn leads to a portfolio of projects and budgetary planning.

The famous adage in architecture, "Form follows Function", can be easily adapted for strategic planning and project management - Scope follows Objectives, Objectives follow Projects, Projects follow Goals, Goals follow Strategy, and Strategy follows Mission and Mission follows Vision.

Thus a project scope must ultimately relate to objectives, goals, strategy, mission and vision of an enterprise. A typical strategic planning cycle consists of the following steps:

- Define the organization's vision and objectives
- Conduct an environment scan pertaining to market trends
- Perform a SWOT analysis
- Do a needs analysis and formulate expected results
- Develop key strategic outcomes and enablers
- Map projects against strategic outcomes and impact on client operations
- Prepare implementation plan, budgets & schedule of projects for each department

The lack of a well defined process for strategic planning often results in projects that are neither supported nor justified by a business need. Such projects are initiated with considerable hype, hoopla and hysteria only to find that they become "troubled projects" sooner or later, since they are not aligned with an organization's strategic objectives. Project Governance offers an effective solution to ensure the "project to business" alignment.

Project Governance

Project Governance provides a holistic approach to how projects are initiated, evaluated, selected, approved, managed, implemented and closed in an organization. Its purpose is to manage and minimize the impact of organizational politics on projects, and to ensure the use of a consistent and predictable set of processes and common terminology in the enterprise.

It looks at the entire life cycle of a project by having a clearly defined process, and ensures that project priorities are consistent with organizational goals. Governance helps an organization to deal with competitive pressures and politics within the organization, and make decisions based on the overall contribution and value of the project.

Project Governance is usually administered by a management or steering committee that consists of key senior executives drawn from different parts of the organization. The committee's purpose is to deal with the politics, priorities and people constraints of projects, and make decisions based on the project's ROI, strategic alignment and value to the organization.

The committee accomplishes this through a charter which typically includes the following:

- Ensure that major projects in the organization are supported by a Business Case, Justification, and a Business Sponsor

- Ensure that the projects are aligned with the strategic direction and business goals of the organization, and its future technology architecture

- Oversee project priorities and allocation of resources based on the project's overall value and contribution to the organization

- Create an enabling environment for culture change towards a "Projectized" environment

- Support management of change (re process, people and technology) resulting from project implementations

Figure 14

Project Governance Model

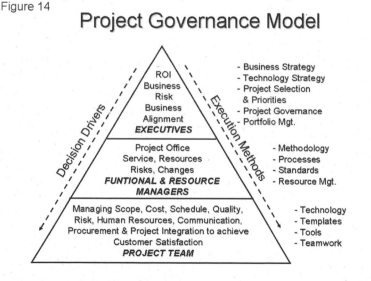

© Dhanu Kothari & Romeo Mitchell 2007

- Oversee that approved projects have an ongoing commitment from project stakeholders

- Conduct ongoing review and approval of projects and status

- Provide timely resolution of strategic issues & conflicts

Figure 14 illustrates the ideal scope of Project Governance including business and technology strategy, portfolio management, project management office (PMO) and project management methodology.

Project Portfolio Management (PPM)

Project Portfolio Management (PPM) is the critical link that integrates the Idealism of Project Governance with the varying demands and needs of individual projects in an organization. Governance is focused on optimizing benefits and value from competing projects, while projects are associated with cost, schedule, quality and deliverables as they apply to their specific objectives. Project Portfolio Management bridges the gap between overall governance and individual projects.

A project may be initiated for a variety of reasons, and its objectives may be driven by goals, perspectives and priorities that are not always consistent across the organization. There may be duplication of effort due to similar or overlapping objectives among projects proposed by different departments, or they might have conflicting goals, objectives and agenda leading to the adage "The right hand doesn't know what the left hand is doing". PPM facilitates the process for getting the right projects into the pipeline.

Projects are also perceived differently by various levels and functions of the organization, and therefore, identified with their specific roles in approving, allocating or administering the project. For an executive, a project is all about strategies, alignment, goals and budgets; for a manager, it's about resources, processes and progress; for the Project Manager it's all about getting work done within the triple constraints of scope, time and cost with the primary focus on milestones, deliverables, issues and risks. These varying perspectives can cause havoc on assigning priorities, approving projects, allocating resources and advancing the causes for projects.

125

A department that has a high portion of the annual budget can wield undue influence and leverage while another with a lower budget may have little influence for getting its projects into the pipeline. Similarly, infrastructure type of projects are identified with major costs and therefore, seen as a drain on the limited financial resources of the organization, while those having a positive impact on costs, revenues or customer service are seen as contributing directly to the business.

It is no wonder that projects associated with revenue and profit usually get the highest priority, and they tend to skew the approval process in their favour, as opposed to those that are seen as major costs. PPM optimizes the process for selecting projects and developing a comprehensive and achievable portfolio based on an organization's strategies, constraints, priorities and realities.

The functional organization that facilitates and guides the execution of PPM processes, ensures consistent planning for individual projects, and implements standards and methodologies for managing projects across the organization is known as the Enterprise Project Management Office (EPMO) or simply as the PMO in smaller organizations. To be successful, a PMO must have the support and commitment of senior executives, and its enthusiastic acceptance by Project Managers and project teams.

A PMO is not a substitute for lack of basic project management discipline and skills, and it is not a "silver bullet" solution for organizations plagued with troubled projects. For the PMO to be effective and successful, there must be genuine buy-in by all concerned, and the organization must have reached a certain level of maturity with respect to acceptance of and adherence to, sound Project Management methodologies and practices.

Role of the Enterprise PMO (EPMO)

EPMO is the functional unit that administers project governance, portfolio management and project management discipline across the organization. As such, EPMOs are associated with varying degrees of scope, mandate and responsibility depending on the culture, size, type and maturity of the organization.

They develop and implement a common set of policies, processes and tools that cover the entire life cycle of a project from its initiation to completion and ongoing operation. They train and coach Project Managers, and provide management oversight with respect to budgets, risks and schedules and documentation for major projects. Finally, they facilitate the flow of information, make problems visible, seek consensus-based resolutions and continually improve the project management processes.

EPMOs can achieve all of the above only with a fine balance of authority and responsibility associated with the function. Too much authority without responsibility conveys the impression that it is another level of bureaucracy and a policing function created to make the Project Manager's life miserable! Too much responsibility without authority gets associated with meddling in the affairs of a Project Manager or just another reporting function with no real clout in the organization.

"What is the value of the EPMO and how does it benefit us?" is indicative of the doubts raised by Project Managers. EPMOs have failed too often because they are either perceived as "methodology monsters" or "lame ducks" by the rest of the organization.

Successful EPMOs require a management of change and a cultural shift with respect to the ways an organization manages its projects, and they are associated with the following factors:

- They are fully supported by management as part of its commitment to implementing Project Governance

- They are established for the right reasons, such as advancing the maturity of project management practices, with supporting goals and strategies.

- They are sold to the organization as a value-added function for delivering project value to the business.

- They are driven from the top with genuine management commitment and demanded by the bottom as a proven vehicle for delivering successful projects.

- They are backed by an experienced Program Manager who commands respect for his seniority, skills and savvy in getting things done, and is dedicated to coaching Project Managers.

- They are equipped with the right policies, procedures, methodologies and tools that are perceived to be useful and consistently followed in the organization.

The following table provides a summary of the functions, features and benefits of the EPMO.

Project Governance and the EPMO

EPMO Functions What	EPMO Features How	EPMO Benefits Why
Ensure alignment of projects with business objectives	Integrate Bus. Case into Project Benefits and Org. Strategy	Align projects with strategic objectives
Portfolio Management	Prioritize, integrate and select projects based on ROI and strategic value	Minimize impact of politics; eliminate redundancies and optimize resources
Implement a set of standardized processes, procedures, tools	Adopt a standard methodology with tools and templates	Consistency Predictability Standardization
Review, monitor, report project status with recommendations	Analysis, synthesis and integration of reports	Risk Assessment & Reliable Reporting
Build a knowledge base of lessons learned and best practices	Institute regular audits, debriefing and post implementation reviews	Better "On Time", Budgets, Resourcing and Expectations
Monitor and optimize resource utilization	Maintain Knowledge Base & Repository	Leverage Reuse, Experience and Knowledge
Maintain project portfolio; implement communication & escalation process	Implement Portfolio Project Mgt. process	Resource Capacity & Allocation Mgt.
Report on metrics for project delivery and business value realized	Develop metrics re: PM Maturity, Project Delivery and Value	Develop, Track & Report on Metrics; Gates, Go/No Go
Provide advocacy and "selling" for PMO and Project Management	Coaching, Mentoring and Training for Project Managers	Promote a "Projectized" Culture

15 best practices for recovery

Project Recovery - The A^{10} Model$^©$

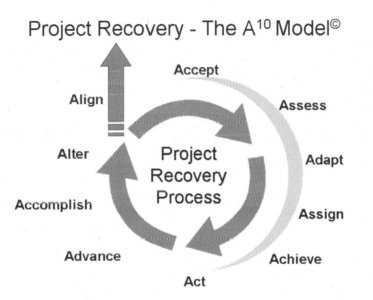

This chapter summarizes the lessons learned and best recommended practices based on the experience of Project Recovery Managers and the application of the AIM - A10 Recovery Methodology. They are presented in three sections that follow the AIM methodology:

- Recovery Start-up - Audit & Plan (A)
- Recovery Implementation - Implement the Plan (I)
- Recovery Follow up - Manage the Transition (M)

No discussion of lessons learned would be complete without a thorough checklist of steps that can be taken to prevent a project failure or the need for a recovery in the first place. Figure 15-A summarizes the lessons learned. A checklist of best practices for basic Project Management follows at the end of the chapter.

Recovery Start-up: Best Practices

1. *Engage the customer*

   There can be no recovery unless the customer is fully committed to the objectives of recovery and ownership of process. The only way to ensure commitment is to have the customer engaged and involved in the process right from the very beginning. Recovery is a joint effort that requires active cooperation between the delivery organization and the customer.

2. *Assess complexity and readiness*

   Gauge the complexity of recovery including project size, organization, culture, management commitment, sponsorship, reporting relationships and the gap between what has been reported and what really exists. Too often, management is not even aware of the need for recovery, or the organization culture may discourage the truth being discussed.

3. *Finalize recovery objectives*

   Clarify the role of the Recovery Manager and scope of recovery; get agreement on objectives; consider alternatives; look for options including redefinition and re-scoping the project, phased deliverables, staggered implementation and accelerated delivery.

4. *Develop a realistic plan*

   A successful recovery is only possible with an achievable plan, and is not based on hoping for the best. Do everything possible to eliminate doubt, despair, fatigue, fear and frustration that the team has already experienced as part of dealing with a troubled project. Plan for success and promise only what you can deliver.

5. *Leverage team knowledge and experience:*

The project owes its troubled state to many factors that are often outside the influence or control of the team. Don't fault the team; instead, build on its experience and expertise whenever possible. Build a team culture based on trusting relationships and collaborative teamwork. Projects by definition change the status quo, and recovery projects add another level of complexity to the change. Incorporate management of change into the recovery plan.

6. *Restructure the team*

Get to know the team members; finalize team structure; ensure that there is a client manager/acceptor assigned to the team. Evaluate individual team member's skills, strengths, weaknesses, commitment and fitness for the assigned role, and make adjustments when necessary. Define roles and responsibilities including those of the Sponsor, Client Manager, Project Manager & the Recovery Manager. It should be especially clear who is driving the bus and who is riding it.

Recovery Implementation: Best Practices

1. *Coach the Project Manager*

Coaching is an integral part of recovery and it takes place while the project is being stabilized. Set up a formal schedule and method for coaching. Make the role of the Recovery Manager explicitly known to everyone - it is an interim role to guide and help the Project Manager to gain control of the project. The Project Manager is still responsible for the project, and implements the recovery plan with advice and guidance of the Recovery Manager.

2. *Improve the Project Environment*

Isolate the team, if necessary, and acquire the right tools for managing everything from requirements to reporting. Review Project Management practices and eliminate unproductive and redundant activities. Why bother doing the same things the same way if they haven't helped in the past? Provide administrative/ clerical help to support the team and offload tasks where possible. Establish a schedule for reporting and reviews, and keep the schedule aggressive, yet achievable.

3. *Sell the Recovery Plan*

To succeed, the project team has to overcome its skepticism and it must believe in the plan, purpose and possibility of recovery. The same goes for the client and stakeholders who are anxious about the project and want the recovery to be completed quickly. In both cases, the Recovery Manager is expected to sell the recovery: first, to the team members to get them motivated and get their enthusiastic support; and second, to management and the client to set their expectations in terms of goals, objectives and process of recovery.

4. *Communicate Effectively*

Institute a culture of open and honest communication within the team and with the client. Tell the news as it is: including the good, the bad and the ugly. It is the lack of crucial and honest communication that caused a troubled project in the first place. Don't delay, diminish or downplay the bad news. Insulate the team from organizational issues, politics and frequent interruptions. Manage information flow and set up a communication plan that outlines the format, flow and frequency of communication.

5. *Deliver "Quick-wins"*

Plan to deliver a series of steady "Quick-wins" that are important and meaningful for the client. They demonstrate progress made in regaining control of the project. They build confidence among the client, Project Manager and the team, and validate the team's commitment to the project. Above all, they help the Project Manager to manage the psychology of the project by focusing on tangible deliverables for the client.

6. Execute with Rigour

Execution is where the rubber meets the road. It includes adhering to standards, implementing consistent processes, documenting details, conducting reviews, managing meetings, tracking progress, reporting status, controlling change, managing issues and escalating them as required . A recovery is doomed to failure in the absence of basic rigour and discipline of Project Management.

Lessons Learned – Best Practices

Projects get late...one day at a time!
Act as an optimist, Manage the risks.
If it's not documented, it doesn't exist!
Think as a pessimist, plan for the risks.
Micro Management is the #1 Killer of projects.
No News is Bad News! Insist on status reports.
One who controls the minutes also controls the project.
Get the team actively involved. It leads to commitment.
Engage the client and manage the client's expectations.
Don't try to solve "world hunger" when scoping a project.
Make expectations clearly known to every team member
Give people responsibility for a deliverable - not an activity!
Focus on the process first, not people - for problem solving.
Responsibilities are delegated: Commitments are accepted.
Decision making is a process; decision taking is an individual act.
Make ground rules known - don't assume that people know them.
Politics is the ability to influence people with savvy and sensitivity.
Purpose of Communication is to advance the project towards completion.
Management decides to take the risk; the Project Mgr. manages the risk.
The Project Mgr. is 100% responsible for success or failure of the project.

Post Recovery: Best Practices

Recovery is completed once the project is stabilized, and the Project Manager is confidently in charge of managing the project to its successful conclusion. Having helped to bring the project back on rails, the Recovery Manager's role shifts to the following activities:

- Provide ongoing coaching to the Project Manager
- Review and monitor management of change with respect to the project
- Influence the organization to adopt Project Governance

The goal here is to ensure that the project doesn't slip back into a recovery mode again, and to help the organization to continually enhance its maturity for delivering successful projects as discussed in the previous chapter.

Preventing Failure – Best Practices

Project Management is defined as the art and science of getting work done with the active cooperation of the customer, stakeholders and the team. It is essentially about making things happen by communicating effectively, dealing with people and managing relationships.

In a recovery environment, Project Management skills are sharply focused and efficiently executed under great pressure and in a very short time. They are summarized below as best practices for managing successful projects and preventing failures.

Follow the Basics - PM 101

1. Understand the basic characteristics of a project as referenced in the PMBOK
2. Validate that the project satisfies the criteria for each characteristic
3. Understand and internalize the functions of Project Management
4. Establish the Project Manager role as the single point of responsibility
5. Promote and adopt formal Project Management practices

Understand Responsibility Vs Authority

1. Recognize constraints of the Project Manager role: 100% responsibility Vs. perceived lack of authority
2. Exercise the implicit authority to do the right thing for the project

3. Consult and communicate with all interested parties; get formal approvals as required
4. Understand the languages and perspectives of Business, Technology and Project Management
5. Develop the recommended skills and competencies for Project Management

Ensure Project Alignment

1. Articulate the project goals in terms of business needs
2. Continually validate that the project is aligned with the organization's business strategies and customer needs
3. Set 4-5 major project objectives that have passed the SMART test. Review, redefine and restate the project objectives to satisfy the SMART criteria (i.e. Specific, Measurable, Achievable, Realistic and Target-driven)
4. Ensure that key players associated with the project have a common understanding of its goals and expectations
5. Review, redefine or terminate the project if there is no business need

Get the Baseline Right

1. Follow the planning, estimating, scheduling process - the schedule is the final product.
2. Get your team involved in the planning process. There are no tools that will do the thinking for you.
3. Get your client and the team involved in the process - it's easier to get their buy-in and enthusiastic support of the final schedule.
4. Invest time and effort into the scheduling exercise - after all, what is critical is how you arrived at the schedule, not the schedule itself.
5. Develop a baseline which is a result of negotiations and commitments regarding resources and other requirements

Scope the Project Clearly

1. Get a handle on the "What" before jumping into the "How"
2. Involve the client and key stakeholders in the requirements definition and project scoping discussions
3. Facilitate the WBS creation process

135

4. Use problem-solving skills and get consensus along the way for each iteration
5. Make WBS the foundation for planning, managing and controlling the project
6. Conduct a maximum of three iterations and you will capture 95% of the scope

Organize Who Does What

1. Follow the four quadrants surrounding the Project Manager role (e.g. Sponsor, Customer, Stakeholders and Team Members), and question rigorously if any of the roles are missing
2. Identify the roles as they relate to your project
3. Describe the responsibilities for each role in the project
4. Identify a specific individual and assign a name for each role, and get agreement on the responsibilities
5. Publish a Project Organization chart indicating the roles and individual names

Develop an Implementation Roadmap

1. Get the client and the project team involved in developing the roadmap
2. Present the roadmap to the client and senior management
3. Identify the critical path and make sure that all members are aware of it
4. Display the roadmap with milestones, critical path and assigned resources
5. Manage the project by monitoring the critical path and milestones

Document Diligently

1. First plan the work, then work the plan
2. Facilitate the planning exercise and conduct three good iterations; you can capture 95% of the input.
3. Establish a Project Workbook and make it available to the project team
4. Have a process for revising and updating the contents of the workbook

5. Educate/Coach the sub-contractor to follow the planning process

Delegate Effectively

1. Develop your network of contacts in the organization
2. Monitor the right indicators for the project
3. Develop, distribute and display RACI/RAM charts
4. Continually validate team member's understanding of responsibilities and commitments
5. Conduct de-briefing sessions throughout the project (e.g. end of phase, significant milestone etc.)

Manage Risks & Uncertainties

1. Identify the top three risks related to TIMO - Technology, Implementation, Management & Organizational considerations for the project
2. Have an up-to-date list of the top three risks that may jeopardize the project over the short term (four weeks) and long term (three months)
3. Prepare a Risk Management Plan based on your mitigation strategy
4. Have a "Ready to Execute" Risk Management plan
5. Include risk funding as part of the project
6. Get the Risk Management plan approved by the Senior Management
7. Make risk review a permanent agenda item in your project review meetings

Manage Costs and Expectations

1. Develop costs based on estimated workdays and productivity
2. Include budget for risk management depending on the risk strategy
3. Monitor the budgeted cost, actual cost and variance by deliverables and milestones
4. Focus on earned value and estimate to complete (ETC) at every major milestone
5. Continually manage the client's expectations by reporting an up-to-date and accurate picture of all costs

Deliver Project & Process Quality

1. Adopt a "process" view of Project Management - Define the processes
2. Adopt the seven quality tools for monitoring project variables
3. Monitor cost of quality - Conformance and non-conformances
4. Strive for "Every deliverable on time, first time every time"
5. Develop a balanced score card for the project; keep it simple
6. Hold Post implementation audits, lessons learned sessions
7. Institute customer satisfaction measures and conduct post-implementation surveys
8. Maintain history of project data for reference and use it
9. Diligently follow the process for managing projects - You cannot improve a process by avoiding it!

Build, Energize & Motivate the Team

1. Practice the 5Rs - Respect, Recognition, Rewards, Rest and Recreation
2. Energize your team and the client
3. Hold open dialogues with team members and the client
4. Follow problem-solving and decision making processes
5. Focus on the final objective with leadership and vision

Communicate to Succeed

1. Issue weekly Project Status reports & Monthly newsletters
2. Have a checklist of deliverables and obtain incremental signoffs
3. Validate that the communication is complete
4. Keep the "macro" view and the big picture visible
5. Provide visuals re project organization, dependency chart, milestone completion etc. and post them in the project war room
6. Maintain perspective - Don't lose sight of the forest for the trees

Succeed with Soft Skills

1. Develop an awareness of the benefit of soft skills among team members
2. Adopt a team process that encourages the use of soft skills

3. Develop and practice soft skills until they are internalized
4. Coach team members to develop and apply soft skills
5. Engage actively in making presentations to client, management and project team

Enhance Professionalism & Training

1. Adopt a process-based methodology and stick to it
2. Conduct methodology training for the project team, clients and stakeholders
3. Provide executive orientation regarding project management, process improvement and regulatory compliance
4. Continually monitor your obligations as a Project Manager
5. Ask for help when faced with situations that may result in compromising one's integrity

The Bottom Line

The lessons learned are grouped into five categories as shown in Figure 15. Catch the "Pot of Gold" with customer focus, executive sponsorship, organizational relationships, collaborative teamwork and process improvement.

Figure 15

"Catch the Rainbow" with
Project Management Best Practices

© Dhanu Kothari & Romeo Mitchell 2007

139

Customer Focus Counts

The sole purpose of a project is to satisfy the client's business and organizational goals and needs. Extraordinary Project Managers go beyond managing projects merely to the client's stated requirements. They focus on understanding their customers' needs, business rationale, desired outcomes and success criteria.

They demonstrate the flexibility required to adapt to the client's changing business environment. Above all, they work with the customer to build a strong working relationship dedicated to achieving success in their projects. The customer comes first!

Sponsorship Leads to Success

Projects need an enthusiastic and committed sponsor to be successful. The sponsor sets the vision, ensures that the project is aligned with the business strategy, and provides organizational support for the Project Manager. Without this support, the Project Manager faces immense challenges in overcoming organizational issues and resistance that are normally associated with a project.

The Project Manager's job is to get the project done, not change the organization or its culture (unless that in itself is within the scope of the project). The sponsor indicates true evidence of management's commitment to the project. Why undertake the project if management isn't serious about it? When it comes to managing successful projects, sponsorship does matter!

Relationships Are Rewarding

Every Project Manager aspires to build a "trusted partner" relationship with clients and stakeholders including vendors, suppliers and sub-contractors. Relationships are crucial to exercising influence and arriving at decisions based on confidence, cooperation and consensus.

Good relationships help us build bridges with others at the emotional level where, in the final analysis, people tend to make most of their decisions. Such relationships thrive on mutual trust based on honesty and integrity. Experienced Project Managers practice an inclusive approach to project management by having the stakeholders' representation in project teams. Building strong relationships has its own rewards for Project managers.

Teams Thrive on Teamwork

Every project is an interesting and challenging endeavour in terms of getting work done with the active and enthusiastic participation of team members. Teams need to be structured and motivated and, most importantly, driven by a mission or purpose.

Teamwork needs to be sustained by leadership that builds on, and promotes mutual respect, responsibility for accomplishment, sense of ownership and empowerment, and genuine recognition and unwavering trust among its members.

The hallmarks of a successful project are a sense of purpose, outstanding teamwork, mutual trust and a feeling of achievement. Project Managers provide leadership to create and build effective teams.

Process Improvement Pays

Just like any other work, Project Management can also be viewed as a series of processes. The processes define how an organization manages its project-related business including the use of standards, definition of phases, delivery of tasks, assessment of risks, and the conduct of management reporting, reviews and approvals.

The quality concept of Supplier, Input, Process, Output and Customer (SIPOC) is as much applicable to Project management processes as it is to any other work process. Project Management entails managing these processes with a focus on the customer and continuous improvement. Adopt a process view of Project Management, analyze and improve the processes, and win with successful projects!

Successful Project Management is built on a solid foundation of customer focus, executive sponsorship, organizational relationships, motivated teams and process orientation. Build your foundation and catch the pot of gold!

16

case study:
a successful recovery

Project Recovery - The A^{10} Model$^©$

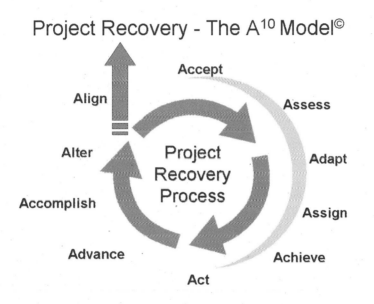

Accept

Align

Assess

Alter

Project
Recovery
Process

Adapt

Accomplish

Assign

Advance

Achieve

Act

In preparation for this case study, the authors interviewed a Project Recovery Manager who was assigned to rescue a complex project in a large multi-national organization, and successfully transformed it into a successful recovery using the conceptual framework of the AIM-A10 recovery methodology. Excerpts from the interview follow.

(Note: Information on project background and recovery events has been modified to protect the client's interest and to make the case study as universal as possible.)

Interviewer: Tell us about the project background.

Project Recovery Manager (PRM): This was a fairly complex infrastructure project undertaken by a multi-national corporation in the financial industry. The objectives of the project were to build a common enterprise network by implementing an integrated WAN/LAN infrastructure for communication.

The business need was to achieve the integration of various Lines of Businesses (LOBs) for the purposes of data sharing, security access and general ease of communication.

The project was "mission critical" since the clients were experiencing a massive growth in their services and, therefore, ever escalating cost of network operations. Furthermore, the fragmented state of their network resulted in constant patchworks, upgrades, breakdowns and failures. Getting the project done was the only alternative.

What was the size of the project?

PRM: The project was initiated as part of a larger Service Level Agreement (SLA) between two divisions- the implementing organization and sponsoring organization. The planned term of the service agreement was 6 years. The infrastructure implementation project was estimated at 20 months. Overall value of the service agreement was around $100M. The infrastructure component consisting of hardware, software and project resources was estimated to be around $25M.

Who were the main players?

PRM: There were several players. To begin with, there was a corporate Project Sponsor who represented the interests of business entities including their product line business units and internal IT departments. The business units were designated as clients for the project. As you can imagine, there were as many clients as the entities - somewhere in the range of 25 primary clients and 65 stakeholders in total.

How about the Project Manager?

PRM: The project was awarded to an external vendor who specialized in implementing infrastructures for integrated communication. The vendor assigned a Project Director to liaise with the Project Sponsor. The Project Director was also responsible for managing multiple sub-projects and vendors for assessment, design, hardware, software, network implementation, switch deployment and migration.

So, how did you get into the picture? What was the problem?

PRM: There were multiple delays and missed milestones on the project. The clients felt that they were misinformed about the project and not kept in the loop. The sponsor was not satisfied with the progress. The reasons and justification given by the Project Director was inadequate, unsubstantiated and unconvincing.

The Project Sponsor sensed that something was seriously wrong with the situation, and decided to bring me in as a Recovery Manager. "I am thinking of firing the Project Manager. Help me sort out the mess and bring the project back on track" was the expectation.

Where did you start? What was the first step?

PRM: I proposed a "Quick Scan" as the first step since it would give me an early appreciation of the complexity and magnitude of the issues. It would also help me to examine if the project could realistically be rescued, and make recommendations to the Project Sponsor accordingly.

During the "Quick Scan", I met with the Sponsor and the Director to validate challenges and concerns regarding communication and lack of progress. I asked them to share with me their perspectives on their roles and the project schedule.

What did you find in the "Quick Scan"?

PRM: I was absolutely surprised at the gap in communication. They couldn't even agree on the schedule since each one had an entirely different document.

The Project Director's schedule, which represented the implementing organization, focused solely on technical aspects of the implementation, whereas the sponsoring organization's schedule dealt solely with the implementation of business processes in client organizations.

Guess what? Both of them had a schedule that they felt was relevant for their purposes, but it wasn't the same one. The end result ... the Project Director was communicating status based on only the technical aspects of the implementation.

Similarly, the Sponsoring organization was only interested in progress relative to the business units and their goals. There was no correlation between the two schedules and there was no common ground for reporting.

What was the reaction of the participants?

PRM: The Project Director was very defensive of the situation, almost in a state of denial, and convinced that he was doing the best job under the circumstances and in accordance with his schedule.

The "Quick Scan" had also given some clues regarding the lack of motivation and low morale among his team members. The Director felt that this could be attributed to the fact that the clients and stakeholders were too business-oriented and they didn't have any appreciation for the technical complexities of such a project.

The Project Sponsor, on the other hand, was leaning towards replacing the Project Manager. He even wondered if I would be interested in taking over the project as the Project Recovery Manager!

Following the "Quick-Scan", what did you decide to do next?

PRM: My immediate goal was to get them to recognize and accept the facts. It seemed to me that the delivery organization (i.e. Project Director) knew that there were major challenges with the project, but played down their significance.

The Project Director viewed the project only as a technical implementation, and the extent of his responsibility as managing the technical component. The Project Sponsor had also felt that the project was in trouble, and had accepted the fact as a result of poor communication.

The biggest challenge was to get the two parties to acknowledge and accept the facts. I met with the delivery team and demonstrated with examples that there was disconnect in communication, and I also got them to acknowledge that there was a significant gap in terms of customer expectations and expected progress.

The Project Manager sincerely believed that the expectation gap was a business problem, and as such, it was "Owned" by the sponsor. "I am responsible for technology. Tough luck if they cannot understand and interpret what I say!" was his attitude towards dealing with the sponsoring organization.

It took a series of three meetings to get them to acknowledge and accept that there was a critical gap in communication and expectations. I recommended a detailed assessment of the situation before taking further action on the project. The stage for a detailed assessment was now set.

What happened during the Assessment?

PRM: Conducting interviews was a significant part of the assessment. I interviewed all the key players - Project Sponsor, Project Director, internal and external stakeholders, Project Managers, Account Managers who sold the project, business unit representatives, executive sponsors and selected foot soldiers from perceived troubled areas of the project.

The interviews were driven by information obtained from the Quick Scan and the objective was to solicit their concerns and experiences ... feeling the pulse, if you will. I asked questions to explore roles, relationships, accountabilities and responsibilities as they saw them. I tried to identify further gaps by asking them about planning, tracking and reporting for the project. Finally, I wanted to get their general perspectives and the level of comfort and confidence on the project.

During the assessment, I reviewed project documents pertaining to contracts, requirements, Statement of Work (SOW), schedules, status reports and general project communication. I reviewed Variance Analysis to validate accuracy and integrity of reporting, and performed a gap analysis with respect to standard Project Management practices.

Were you surprised with the results of the Assessment?

PRM: Yes. There were many surprises. There was a lack on an effective project organization. They weren't aware of the fact that they were dealing with a program consisting of multiple major projects. The complexity of the project was severely under-estimated. The project team was de-motivated and felt that the project was doomed to go on for ever. There was no project plan ... all they had was a schedule!

Project reporting was limited to status and issues based only on technical perspectives. They believed that there was a Program Management Office (PMO); however, it existed only in theory, not in practice. There was no project governance, and they didn't have standard project control tools for change and issue management.

The project was simply taken over by dozens of new issues popping up every day, and it had turned into a frantic issue management exercise. There was significant cost variance in addition to schedule variance - only 4 months worth of work was delivered in 11 months. The concept of Earned Value Analysis (EAV) did not exist for the project.

How did the Assessment end? Do you have any general observations?

PRM: As a result of the Assessment, I delivered a detailed report along with an executive presentation. The report identified major issues, root causes and recommended steps for proceeding with a recovery based on Project Recovery Charter.

My assessment indicated that the Project Director was quite competent in technology, and would benefit by coaching for managing large projects. The recommendations were targeted at coaching the Project Director rather than replacing him.

There are several lessons to be learned:

- Political environment influences people's responses during an assessment. People are often "economical with the truth" and there is no free flow of information. Also, responses from contract employees tend be less reserved and more revealing.

- Perception among team members that they really don't need or can't afford the discipline of Project Management, usually based on the notion, "We only know what we experienced, it worked in the past and we don't need anything more".

- There was an underlying problem - Nobody felt responsible for driving the integrated schedule. There was no single point of responsibility for the overall project. None of the Project Managers had the experience of managing a project of that magnitude, and there was no one else to guide them.

You referred to a Recovery Charter. What is it?

PRM: The Recovery Charter serves two objectives. First, it confirms formal assignment of a Recovery Manager to work in conjunction with the Project Manager. Second, it clearly outlines the objectives of recovery along with roles and responsibilities.

In this case, the Recovery Charter made it clear that my sole objective was to stabilize the project and set up basic Project

Management processes quickly, but not to run it on behalf of the Project Director.

The Project Director was still responsible for managing the project in accordance with the new Project Baseline established during the recovery. It was critical that everyone understood this distinction between a Recovery Charter, a Project Charter and a Project Baseline.

As part of the Recovery Charter, I conducted the following activities:

- Re-evaluated and validated customer requirements with respect to business needs. It was evident that the project didn't have the right individuals who could serve as interfaces and interpreters between business and technical groups

- Appointed "Single Points of Contacts (SPOCs) who functioned as experienced Business Analysts, documented customer's expectations, defined roles and responsibilities for SPOCs, prepared a communication matrix to ensure timely and relevant information flow, and modified status report to reflect both technical and business related progress

- Developed a program structure to facilitate business to program alignment that further extended to project objectives, appointed SPOCs who were responsible for interfacing for multiple projects with technical team and multiple clients.

- Revised the original Project Charter based on results of the above activities.

The biggest challenge was dealing with the large number of business clients who had preferred solutions for their unique needs, and achieving a compromise for a single common solution. The SPOC role was very helpful in this case.

With these activities, I was able to bring the focus of the project back to the clients' business needs. The activities resulted in a revised Project Charter and revised project plans which were presented to senior management for approval and accepted as the "go forward" plan.

It should be noted that the Project Director took the leading role in performing these activities with my guidance. Because of the nature of interactive discussions, we averaged 8-10 meetings a week over a 3 week period. Getting to this point took about 4 weeks since I joined as the Recovery Manager.

So, you have a new Project Charter. What about the Recovery?

PRM: The new Project Charter became the basis for developing a Program/Project organization structure, a PMO management plan, and a new recovery baseline. That required several meetings with the Project Director, Sponsor, seven Project Managers and five SPOCs to clarify everyone's role, relationships and responsibilities. We also included Subject Matter Experts (SMEs) to serve as coaches in specialized areas.

When the final plan was ready, we held a recovery kickoff meeting attended by senior management and the project team. We presented the recovery baseline and a formal plan for communication that included weekly review meetings, status reports, escalation processes and change management. The Project Director also became the chief SPOC for the project which meant a significant change in his role.

The experience reinforced the basic principles and best practices for working with people: Hold frequent one-on-one discussions to build trust, focus on process related issues rather than people, work directly with the affected individuals, and get them to actively participate in planning their work and developing targets.

How did you plan for the Recovery?

PRM: We focused on achieving goals by setting small, frequent and intermediate targets that were meaningful to the clients. We created a revised master schedule, and acquired tracking tools to help us manage deliverables. We created a deployment activity matrix for each business unit that included both technical and business activities.

As part of standardizing Project Management processes, we formalized the approval process, implemented templates for reporting, and hired a Program Administrator to assist the team. We set micro targets and developed an inch-stone plan both at the program and project levels.

The plan resulted in micro schedules that were used for expediting critical activities for technology groups and the business units. The targets were set from a daily to maximum weekly intervals in collaboration with Project Managers. The inch-stone plan had to be developed in parallel with the master schedule which was evolving.

Tell us more about executing the Recovery Plan. What did you do differently?

PRM: The ability to act consistently and decisively is crucial for executing the recovery plan. That means ensuring that everything takes place like clock work. We set up a weekly timetable of events. We had to make decisions on a daily basis, often they had to be taken right away and their consequences evaluated immediately.

To prevent piling up of issues, we insisted that the clients assign someone to coordinate access to the right individual who had decision making authority. An issue was not allowed to linger on for too long. If it was not resolved within a week, it was escalated to executive steering committee for resolution during the weekly meeting.

The general principle was to escalate issues to the point of resolution and empowerment. This meant that we had 24x7 access to key decision makers including the sponsor, and it was understood that we had to be quick and decisive.

We introduced a standard reporting template to ensure consistency content, format and style of reporting. Working with the team, we developed ground rules and processes for the team, and made sure everyone knew them and the consequences of ignoring them. We also worked with suppliers and sub-contractors to ensure that they understood the recovery plan and were committed to fulfilling their part during recovery.

How about project communications?

PRM: Communication is the key to achieving a successful recovery. My role as a Recovery Manager, mostly consisted of coaching the team and implementing right processes for effective communication. We developed a Communication Matrix that summarized responsibilities, accountabilities and deliverables for the recovery itself, and prepared a detailed one for subsequent management of the project.

The effectiveness and usefulness of the matrix was checked regularly to ensure that the communication strategy was working. I knew it was working well when the relationship between the business and technical sides of the project started showing improvements, and senior management expressed satisfaction with the quality and reliability of information.

Since meetings were a key part of communication, we established a coaching program for Project Managers so that they could run effective meetings. There were a series of business, technical and executive update meetings held weekly. Only those whose presence was necessary and required were invited to participate. Minutes of meetings had to be published within one working day and they were sent out from the Project Director's office.

Visual management was central to our communication strategy. There was a recovery war room with an impressive display of an implementation roadmap, charts and graphs showing milestones, critical activities, work packages and an up to date list of deliverables and signoffs etc. The Program Administrator was the central coordinator for information, and kept everything up-to-date including the big picture, reporting templates, and various logs for Changes, Issues and Action Items.

You mentioned earlier that your job as a Recovery Manager was to bring stability to the project. How did you know that you had achieved stability?

PRM: I see stability from two perspectives. First, the Client and the Sponsoring organization must believe that the project has been turned around and appropriate steps have been taken to assure its successful completion. Second, the Project Manager and the delivery team must feel confident that they can deliver the project as per the revised Project Charter and Baseline.

Here are the key indicators that I used as an "acid test" for determining stability:

- Delivery team has consistently demonstrated that micro and macro targets set up for recovery are being met.

- Tools and processes for tracking and reporting are being used, and the client is satisfied that what is being reported is accurate and reliable.

- Micro-management of the team is no longer required.

- Project Managers are following standard methodology and processes for Project Management.

- Sponsoring organization and client executives recognize that the Project Director is gaining control of the project.

- Client organization is satisfied that there are predictable processes and routines established for the project, and that they are working.

- Project status reports, both from the Client's and team's perspectives, have been consistently positive for a period of time.

- There is an improvement in the level of mutual trust among the key players, and the client's expression of general satisfaction as a result of recovery.

- There is agreement between the delivery and client organizations on the revised Project Charter and Baseline Schedule.

As a Recovery Manager, my role was to enable the Project Director to regain control of the project. When it was agreed that the criteria for stability were met, it was time to begin the process of setting a new direction for the project, transitioning and withdrawing from the project. I had to get ready for my next assignment … to rescue another project!

What did you do to change direction of the project?

PRM: The change of direction was achieved slowly over a period of time. Starting with mutual agreement for coaching, I made sure that the Project Director was gaining confidence and improving skills required to manage the project.

We held debriefing meetings to discuss what was said, how it was communicated, if it failed or succeeded, what were the strengths and shortcomings, and what skills needed to be improved as a result. The coaching encompassed all aspects of people, process and technology issues related to the project.

As we started seeing positive indicators of stability, we reviewed and agreed that the necessary processes and tools were in place, the processes were understood and followed, and everything was working well. We validated the team's confidence for delivering the project and agreed on a schedule for my withdrawal from the project.

By this time the project organization was fine-tuned and everyone had settled well into their new roles. The Project Administrator and the project team were reporting directly to the Project Director.

There was some resistance to the change of guard, as one would expect in a project of this size. Our strategy was to

155

isolate the resistance, understand the reasons behind it, and work with the individuals concerned.

Too many "troubled" projects are waiting for a recovery. What can be done to prevent this situation?

PRM: Learn from experience and follow the basics of Project Management. It is as simple as that. For the recovery itself, I suggest the following:

- Archive all project recovery tools and templates
- Conduct a final validation of ongoing implementation activities.
- Follow up with a de-brief of recovery
- Share the lessons learned and
- Continually improve your processes based on the de-brief

Sharing the lessons learned solely isn't going to do anything unless we decide to act. This is the crucial point where organizations are ill-prepared, and therefore, keep going through the cycle of recovery over and over again. Here is what can be done to break the cycle:

- Establish Program Governance
- Adopt Project Portfolio Management (PPM)
- Implement a Program Management Office (PMO)
- Standardize processes for Project Management
- Enhance communication skills of project resources

One final question - How would you describe a Recovery Manager?

PRM: First and foremost, a Recovery Manager is a highly experienced Project Manager who has a track record of delivering successful projects. She is respected by colleagues for expertise, innovation, networking, risk taking and outstanding communication, facilitation and relationship building skills.

The ability to dive quickly into complex situations, apply a wide range of analytical skills, and focus on real problems is absolutely essential. Integrity in dealing with all project participants is a must, as is the ability to inspire confidence.

Above all, the Recovery Manager must be action-oriented, intensely focused and genuinely interested in coaching and mentoring activities. After all, the essence of a successful recovery lies in coaching and enabling the Project Manager to regain control of the project!

appendix

The following tables summarize the application and deployment of various tools and techniques for recovery.

☑	Introduction, creation and use for data gathering
●	On-going application, adjustment, refinement & reference
*	Illustrated tools & Techniques

A10 Techniques Application Matrix

Techniques			A			I				M		
		00	A01	A02	A03	A04	A05	A06	A07	A08	A09	A10
01*	Conduct Earned Value Analysis		☑	☑	●	●	●					
02	Conduct Legal / Contractual Analysis		☑	●	●	●						
03	Conduct Project Review Snapshot		☑	●	●	●						
04	Gather Data & Information Through Interviews		☑	●	●	●	●					
05	Conduct Project Document Reviews		☑	●	●	●						
06	Conduct Health Check Assessment (Questionnaire)			☑		●	●	●			●	
07	Build Assessment Plan For Deep Dive			☑	●	●						
08	Conduct "Deep Dive"			☑	●		●					
09	Use The Best Practice Questionnaire			☑						●	●	
10	Create Recovery Kick-off Agenda				☑	●						
11	Apply Project Organizational Modeling			☑		●	●					
12	Conduct Project Requirements Assessment			☑								
13	Conduct Barrier Identification & Analysis			☑	●	●						
14*	Conduct SWOT Analysis			☑				●	●	●	●	
15	Conduct Risk Analysis/ Planning/ Monitoring			☑	●	●	●	●	●	●		
16	Conduct Technical Coaching Needs Analysis			☑		●	●	●			●	●
17	Conduct PM Coaching Needs Analysis			☑		●	●	●			●	●
18	Establish Post Recovery Baseline									☑	●	
19	Conduct Formal Turnover & Sign-off									☑	●	

A10 Tools Deployment Matrix

Tool Type		00	A			I				M		
			A01	A02	A03	A04	A05	A06	A07	A08	A09	A10
01*	PIQS	☑	●	●								
02*	BCQS		☑	●	●							
03	PCQS		☑	●	●							
04	CSQS		☑	●	●							
05	Go/ No-Go Decision		☑	●	●		●		●			
06	Recovery Success Checklist		☑			●	●			●		●
07	Recovery Charter	☑		●	●	●			●			
08	Stakeholder Analysis		☑			●		●			●	●
09	Stakeholder Satisfaction Survey		☑			☑			☑		☑	
10	Cause & Effect Analysis			☑	●		●	●				
11*	Variance Analysis Slippage Tracking Assessment			☑	●	●	●					
12	Barrier Identification & Analysis			☑	●	●						
13*	Force Field Analysis			☑				●	●			
14	Gap Analysis			☑	●				●			
15	Recovery Plan				☑	●	●	●	●			
16	Project Recovery Transition Checklist									☑	●	
17	"Deep Dive" Assessment Plan			☑	●	●	●					
18	Post Recovery Baseline								☑			
19	Recovery Kick-off Agenda				☑	●						
20	Technical Coaching Needs Assessment				☑					●	●	
21	PM Coaching Needs Assessment				☑					●	●	
22	Coaching Plan				☑					●	●	●
23	Lessons Learned									☑	●	●
24	Program Governance											☑
25	Project Recovery Roadmap			☑		●	●	●	●			
26	Project Health Check			☑	●							
27	RACI Chart					☑	●	●	●			
28	Transition Plan										☑	●
29	Transition Checklist										☑	●
30	Brainstorming			☑			●	●				

#	Tool											
31	Project Team Focus Worksheet				☑	●	●					
32	Flow Charting			☑	●	●						
33	Multi-voting (Consensus Builder)						☑	●				
34	Prioritization Matrix				☑	●	●	●	●			
35	Relationship Diagram			☑	●							
36	State Change Identify/ Analysis & Action								☑	●	●	●
37	Project Human Resources Analysis			☑		●			●		●	
38*	SWOT Analysis			☑		●		●	●			

Project Initial Quick Scan (PIQS)

General Description of the Tool

The PIQS tool is used by the PRM to quickly gain an appreciation and understanding of the project/ program in terms of its characteristics. This is a precursor to the application of the A10 methodology and acts as critical input to the Recovery Charter produced by the PRM. This is typically done on the first day of the of the Project Recovery Manager's involvement.

PIQS			
Customer			
Project Title			
Brief Description of the project:			
Perceived problem areas:			
Business to project Alignment:		Yes	No
Internal enabler		☐	☐
Revenue producer		☐	☐
Project constraints:			
Fixed price		☐	☐
Absolute deadline schedule		☐	☐
Relative deadline schedule		☐	☐
Project Exposure:	High	Medium	Low
Urgency	☐	☐	☐
Priority	☐	☐	☐
Risk	☐	☐	☐
Technology Influence	☐	☐	☐
Complexity	☐	☐	☐
Political sensitivity	☐	☐	☐
HR involvement	☐	☐	☐
General Comments:			

Use of the Tool

- ☑ Prior to producing the Recovery Charter.
- ☑ To gain a quick understanding of the state of the project.
- ☑ Input to PRM engagement.
- ☑ To build a strategy towards A1 process.

Project Characteristics Quick Scan (PCQS)

General Description of the Tool

The PCQS tool is used by the PRM to build on the information gathered from the PIQS. The objective is to capture more detailed information about the project attributes. This involves engaging the project manager and the project team. At the end of this exercise the PRM should have a comprehensive understand of the vision, mission, goals and objectives of the project.

PCQS				
Customer				
Project Title				
Project Mission, Vision & Goals:				
Project Objectives: 1. 2.				
Major Areas of Risk Exposure: 1. 2.				
Complexity Attributes				
Attribute	**Description**	**High**	**Medium**	**Low**
Technical		☐	☐	☐
Implementation		☐	☐	☐
Management		☐	☐	☐
Organizational		☐	☐	☐
Checklist				
Item	**Description**		**Yes**	**No**
1			☐	☐
2			☐	☐
3			☐	☐
4			☐	☐
General Information:				

Use of the Tool

☑ Gather data and information in support of A1 actions.
☑ To gain an in-depth understanding of the project.

Project Standards Compliance Quick Scan (SCQS)

General Description of the Tool

The SCQS tool is used by the PRM to evaluate whether the Project Manager has applied best practices. The objective is to identify any potential gaps and to use that information to adjust and help bridge the standards gap. Typical SCQS form:

SCQS
Customer
Project Title
Initiating Standards: 1. Does a project charter exist? ☐ Yes ☐ No   2. Are all key stakeholders identified and roles determined? ☐ Yes ☐ No   3. Is the project in support of a specific business case? ☐ Yes ☐ No   4. Are there clear and unambiguous requirements? ☐ Yes ☐ No   5. Is there a written scope statement? ☐ Yes ☐ No

Planning Standards:
 6. Is there a detailed baseline plan? ☐ Yes ☐ No
 7. Is the project schedule developed using a scheduling tool? ☐ Yes ☐ No
 8. Does the project plan contain the various sections:
      a. Business justification? ☐ Yes ☐ No
      b. Business goals & objectives? ☐ Yes ☐ No
      c. Project goals & objectives? ☐ Yes ☐ No
      d. Detailed scope description? ☐ Yes ☐ No
      e. Communication plan/ communication matrix? ☐ Yes ☐ No
      f. Project control plan and CR process and forms? ☐ Yes ☐ No
      g. Project risk management plan? ☐ Yes ☐ No
      h. Project financial plan and cost tracking? ☐ Yes ☐ No
      i. Project acceptance criteria? ☐ Yes ☐ No
 9. Was the plan presented to the key stakeholders? ☐ Yes ☐ No

Execution Standards: 10. Progress reports: Planned, actual, major milestones etc? ☐ Yes ☐ No   11. Roles & Responsibility charts? ☐ Yes ☐ No   12. Variance analysis reports? ☐ Yes ☐ No
Monitoring & Control Standards: 13. Change control processes? ☐ Yes ☐ No   14. Issues, decisions, actions, change, risk logs? ☐ Yes ☐ No

Use of the Tool
☑ Gather data and information in support of A1 actions.
☑ Help identify gaps in PM competency.
☑ To gain an in-depth understanding of the project.

Project Variance Tracking Analysis

General Description of the Tool

This tool is used by the PRM to build a micro plan related to the troubled areas of the project. It is specifically designed to capture and analyze activities during a one week period in order to assess variances. This will allow the PRM to develop recovery strategies and alternate ways to expedite the work. Also it allows the project team and Project Manager to appreciate the factors impacting the specific activities.

Planned		Actual		Notes:					
				PVASTA					
Item	Budget		Activity Day					Schedule	
No.	P	A	1	2	3	4	5	P	A
1								2	3
2								1	2
3								2	2
4								2	2
5								1	1
6								2	TBD
SUM									
CUM									
PV									
AC									
EV									
Notes:									

Use of the Tool

☑ Gather data and information during A2 and apply the results to subsequent phases.
☑ To gain an in-depth understanding of the project resource performance.
☑ Used during deep dive exercises.
☑ Input to rectifying troubled areas.

Project Force Field Analysis

General Description of the Tool

This tool is used by the PRM to identify opposing forces acting on the project that may either support the path to success or hinder the path to success. The information gathered through this tool will help plan, implement, monitor and deal with changes in those forces. It allows the PRM to focus on the areas with the greatest benefits and reduce the impact to the project of those areas with the greatest detriment.

Current State (Opposing)

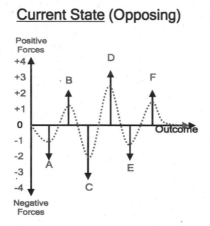

Future State (Neutralized)

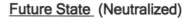
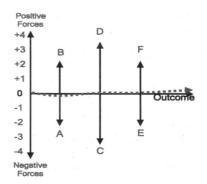

List of Detriments		List of Benefits	
1		1	
2		2	
3		3	
4		4	

Use of the Tool

☑ Allows the RPM to visualize the potential implications of various forces.
☑ Priorities on actions can be addressed.
☑ Data and information can be aligned to the project lifecycle.
☑ The information can be used as input into the change process.

Project Process Flow Charting

General Description of the Tool

The PRM uses flow charts to identify potential areas of problems particularly between the project and the on-going business processes. For example the business approval process may not be very clear to the Project Manager and as a consequence the project is continuously impacted by business decision delays. It can also be used to redesign current processes in order to make them more efficient. This tool is used effectively to determine relationships between organizational entities, mapping out cross functional activities and rationalizing the flow of work.

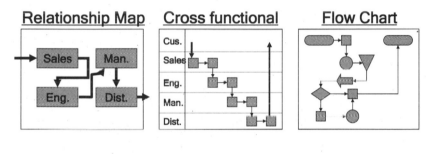

Use of the Tool

☑ To identify human resources relationship.
☑ To determine human resources hiring requirements.
☑ To organizing the work
☑ Use to clarifying roles and contributions.
☑ Identifying improvement opportunities.
☑ Measuring performance.

recommended reading

1. Albrecht, Karl. *Social Intelligence* - *The New Science of Success*. San Francisco: Jossey-Bass (Wiley) 2006 ISBN 0-7879-7938-4

2. Aranda, Eileen and Aranda, Luis. *TEAMS - Structure, Process, Culture and Politics.* New Jersey: Prentice Hall 1998 ISBN 0-13-494584-0

3. Barkley, Bruce and Saylor, James. *Customer-Driven Project Management*. New York: McGraw-Hill 2000 ISBN 0-07-136982-1

4. Block, Robert. *The Politics of Projects.* New Jersey: Prentice Hall 1983 ISBN 0-13-685553-9

5. Bossidy, Larry and Charan, Ram. *Execution: The Discipline of Getting Things Done*, Crown Business, 2002.

6. Brooks, Frederick. *The Mythical Man Month* - Essays on Software Engineering. Massachusetts: Addison-Wesley 1978 ISBN 0-201-00650-2

7. Cagle, Ronald. *Blueprint for Project Recovery - A Project Management Guide* ISBN 0-8144-0766-8

8. Christopher Leadership Course. *Confidence!* New York: The Lumen Institute 1996

9. Craig, Malcolm. *Thinking Visually*. New York: Continuum 2000 ISBN 0-8264-4833-X

10. Hooks, Ivy and Farry, Kristin. *Customer-Centred Products* - *Creating Successful Products through Smart Requirements Management.* New York: American Management Association 2001 ISBN 0-8144-0568-1

11. Jalote, Pankaj. *Software Project management in Practice.* Addison-Wesley (Pearson Education) 2000 ISBN 0-201-73721-3

12. Kothari, Dhanu. Rainbows and Ratholes: Best Practices for Managing Successful Projects. D2i Consulting, Unionville, ON 2006. ISBN 0-97804-69000-1

13. Leeds, Dorothy. *The Seven Powers of Questions.* New York: Berkley Publishing 2000 ISBN 0-399-52614-5

14. Liker, Jeffrey. *The Toyota Way.* New York: McGraw Hill 2004 ISBN 0-07-139231-9

15. McConnell, Steve. *Rapid Development: Taming Wild Software Schedules.* Microsoft Press Redmond, WA. ISBN: 1-55615-900-5.

16. Murphy, James. *Flawless Execution.* New York: Harper Collins 2005 ISBN 0-06-076049-4

17. Patterson, Kerry et al. *Crucial Conversations: Tools for Talking when Stakes are High.* McGraw-Hill ISBN 0071401946

18. Project Management Institute. *A Guide to the Project Management Body of Knowledge.* Pennsylvania: Project Management Institute 2000 ISBN 1-880410-23-0

19. Scholtes, Peter, Joiner, Brian and Streibel, Barbara. *The TEAM Handbook.* Wisconsin: Oriel Publications 2003 ISBN 1-884731-26-0

20. Summers, Donna. *Quality Management - Creating and Sustaining Organizational Effectiveness.* New Jersey: Pearson Prentice Hall 2005 ISBN 0-13-262643-8

21. White Papers: Griffin-Tate Group: Project Recovery
    Univ. of California Davis: Project Recovery Management
    Univ. of Texas: Project Recovery Techniques
    University of Washington: Managing Project Complexities
    Oklahoma State Univ: Project Recovery Management

index